VIETNAM

Maurice Isserman

A PERIGEE BOOK

A Perigee Book
Published by The Berkley Publishing Group
200 Madison Avenue
New York, NY 10016

Copyright © 1995 by Maurice Isserman
Book design by Irving Perkins Associates
Cover design by Dale Fiorillo
Cover illustration courtesy of the Bettmann Archives

First edition: November 1995

Published simultaneously in Canada.

Library of Congress Cataloging-in-Publication Data

Isserman, Maurice.
  Witness to war : Vietnam / Maurice Isserman.—1st ed.
      p.   cm.
  "A Perigee book."
  ISBN 0-399-52162-3 (pbk.)
  1. Vietnamese Conflict, 1961–1975—United States.   I. Title.
DS558.I87   1995
959.704′3373—dc20   95-11408
                                                                       CIP

Printed in the United States of America

10   9   8   7   6   5   4   3   2   1

This book is printed on acid-free paper.

CONTENTS

Vietnam

CHAPTER 1

UNITED STATES INVOLVEMENT in Vietnam developed gradually over a period of three decades. In 1940 Vietnam was a colony of France, and had been since the late 19th century. But at the start of the Second World War, the Japanese took over Vietnam. The Viet Minh, a Communist-led Vietnamese independence movement, launched a resistance campaign against both the Japanese occupiers and the French colonialists. With the defeat of Japan in the war, the French sought to restore their rule in Vietnam. Viet Minh leader Ho Chi Minh appealed to the United States to back the cause of an independent Vietnam. President Franklin Delano Roosevelt had expressed sympathy for the idea of Vietnamese independence during the war. But his successor, Harry Truman, was preoccupied with the growing confrontation with the Soviet Union. Ho Chi Minh came to be regarded as simply another pawn of Moscow. The United States backed French attempts to stamp out the Viet Minh, and by 1954 was paying for 80% of the French war effort.

1

The French surrender at Dienbienphu in the spring of that year brought what would later be called the First Indochinese War to an end. An international conference held in Geneva arranged for the temporary division of Vietnam into two zones. Ho Chi Minh's Communists ruled in the north, while the anti-Communist government of Ngo Dinh Diem ruled in the south. Many anti-Communist refugees fled to the south, aided by an American boatlift. Diem soon declared South Vietnam an independent republic, and refused to hold elections to reunify the country. President Dwight Eisenhower sent several hundred American military advisers, and millions of dollars in economic and military aid, to shore up Diem's unpopular regime in the 1950s. A Communist-inspired resistance movement developed in Vietnam's countryside, which by the late 1950s was receiving some aid from North Vietnam. Although few Americans could find Vietnam on a map in 1960, the United States was being drawn into the Vietnamese civil war.

PRELUDE,
1941–1960

Dear fellow-countrymen!

Since France was defeated by Germany, its power has completely collapsed. Nevertheless, with regard to our people, the French rulers have become even more ruthless in carrying out their policy of exploitation, repression and massacre. . . . The hour has struck! Raise aloft the banner of insurrection and lead the people throughout the country to overthrow the Japanese and the French! The sacred call of the Fatherland is resounding in our ears; the ardent blood of our heroic predecessors is seething in our hearts! . . .

The Vietnamese revolution will certainly triumph!

> —*Letter by Ho Chi Minh to the Vietnamese people on the founding of the Viet Nam Independence League [Viet Nam Doc Lap Dong Minh Hoi, or as it was better known, the Viet Minh], June 6, 1941.*

I saw [British ambassador to the United States, Lord] Halifax last week and told him quite frankly that it was perfectly true

May 10, 1941. Ho Chi Minh founds the Viet Minh (Vietnam Independence League) to coordinate resistance against the Japanese occupiers and French colonial authorities in Vietnam. . . . .

3

that I had, for over a year, expressed the opinion that Indo-China should not go back to France, but that it should be administered by an international trusteeship . . . [T]he case of Indo-China is perfectly clear. France has milked it for one hundred years. The people of Indo-China are entitled to something better than that.

—President Franklin Delano Roosevelt, memo to Secretary of State Cordell Hull, January 24, 1944.

The President said he is much concerned about the brown people in the East. He said that there are 1,100,000,000 brown people. In many eastern countries they are ruled by a handful of whites and they resent it. Our goal must be to help them achieve independence—1,100,000,000 potential enemies are dangerous. He said he included the 450,000,000 Chinese in that. He then added, Churchill doesn't understand this. The President said he thought we might have some difficulties with France in the matter of colonies. I said that I thought that was quite probable and it was also probable that the British would use the French as a "stalking horse." I asked the President if he had changed his mind on French Indochina . . . He said no, he had not changed his ideas: that French Indochina and New Caledonia should be taken from France and put under a trusteeship. The President hesitated a moment and then said—Well if we can get the proper pledge from France to assume for herself the obligations of a trustee, then I would agree to France retaining these colonies with the proviso that independence was the ultimate goal. I asked the President if he would settle

... **December 1944.** The Viet Minh launched armed attacks against French outposts ....

for dominion status. He said no—it must be independence. He said that is to be the policy, and you can quote it in the State Department.

—President Franklin D. Roosevelt, conversation with Charles Taussig, State Department adviser, March 15, 1945.

"All men are created equal. They are endowed by their Creator with certain inalienable rights; among these are Life, Liberty, and the pursuit of Happiness."

This immortal statement was made in the Declaration of Independence of the United States of America in 1776. In a broader sense, this means: All the people on the earth are equal from birth, all the peoples have a right to live, to be happy and free. . . . [F]or more than eighty years, the French imperialists, abusing the standard of Liberty, Equality, and Fraternity, have violated our Fatherland and oppressed our fellow-citizens. . . . We are convinced that the Allied nations which . . . have acknowledged the principles of self-determination and equality of nations, will not refuse to acknowledge the independence of Vietnam. . . . For these reasons, we, members of the Provisional Government of the Democratic Republic of Vietnam, solemnly declare to the world that Vietnam has the right to be a free and independent country—and in fact is so already. The entire Vietnamese people are determined to mobilize all their physical and mental strength, to sacrifice their lives and property in order to safeguard their independence and liberty.

—Vietnam Declaration of Independence, written by Ho Chi Minh and delivered as a speech by him on September 2, 1945.

. . . **September 2, 1945.** Ho Chi Minh proclaims Vietnamese independence at a rally in Hanoi. . . . .

I avail myself of this opportunity to thank you and the people of the United States for the interest shown by your representatives at the United Nations Organization in favor of the dependent peoples.

Our VIETNAM people, as early as 1941, stood by the Allies' side and fought against the Japanese and their associates, the French colonialists. . . . [We] request of the United States as guardians and champions of World Justice to take a decisive step in support of our independence.

What we ask has been graciously granted to the Philippines. Like the Philippines our goal is full independence and full cooperation with the UNITED STATES. We will do our best to make this independence and cooperation profitable to the whole world.

—Ho Chi Minh letter to President Harry S. Truman, February 16, 1946.

It must be the policy of the United States to support free peoples who are resisting attempted subjugation by armed minorities or outside pressure.

—President Harry S. Truman, announcing the "Truman Doctrine," March 12, 1947.

[T]he Kremlin has no compunction about retreating in the face of superior force . . . Its political action is a fluid stream which moves constantly, wherever it is permitted to move, toward a

---

. . . **September 24, 1945.** General Jacques Philippe Leclerc, French military commander in Vietnam, arrives in Saigon, announcing, "We have come to reclaim our inheritance" . . . **December 19, 1946.** After a year of abortive negotiations and sporadic violence, the first Indochina War begins between the Viet Minh and French . . . .

given goal. Its main concern is to make sure that it has filled every nook and cranny available to it in the basin of world power. But if it finds unassailable barriers in its path, it accepts these philosophically and accommodates itself to them. The main thing is that there should always be pressure, increasing pressure, toward the desired goal . . . In these circumstances it is clear that the main element of any United States policy toward the Soviet Union must be that of a long-term, patient but firm and vigilant containment of Russian expansive tendencies.

—*George F. Kennan, Director of U.S. State Department's Policy Planning Staff, "The Sources of Soviet Conduct,"* Foreign Affairs, *July 1947.*

The French Foreign Minister and I have just had an exchange of views on the situation in Indochina and are in general agreement both as to the urgency of the situation in that area and as to the necessity for remedial action. . . . The United States Government, convinced that neither national independence nor democratic evolution exists in any area dominated by Soviet imperialism, considers the situation to be such as to warrant its according economic aid and military equipment to the Associated States of Indochina and to France in order to assist them in restoring stability and permitting these states to pursue their peaceful and democratic development.

—*Statement of policy by U.S. Secretary of State Dean Acheson, May 8, 1950.*

. . . **May 8, 1950.** U.S. Secretary of State Dean Acheson announces agreement to provide arms assistance to the French Associated States of Indochina. . . **August 3, 1950.** 35-member U.S. Military Assistance Advisory Group (MAAG) arrives in Vietnam. . . **December 23, 1950.** United States signs Mutual Defense Assistance Agreement with France and French Associated States of Indochina to provide military aid; by 1954 the United States will be paying for almost 80% of the French war effort . . . .

I interviewed survivors from the border posts. The basic story was always the same. Some of these forts had 350, 400 men. The walls were thick, with parapets, like in a Foreign Legion movie. . . . But the forts were separated by great distances from any support. They were sitting out there all by themselves. The French had very few helicopters and almost no air force. . . . So these guys couldn't call for reinforcements. They had to sit there and fight. If they won, they won, and if they died, they died.

The Viet Minh would attack around midnight. First they'd fire a barrage of heavy mortars . . . It was usually very accurate, because they had a good idea of where your positions were. They infiltrated the forts. All the forts had servants, and the servants came from outside. So they knew where the machine guns were, where the mortars were, where the towers were. They would zero in.

The Legionnaires would get to their defensive positions. They'd look out and see masses of soldiers in palm hats. The helmets of the Viet Minh were made out of palm leaves, a thatched helmet like a pith helmet. It wasn't any good against a bullet, but it was their uniform. You'd see thousands of these guys out there. Usually the first line of defense was barbed wire. The Communists would come with bamboo ladders that they'd put on top of the barbed wire. Your machine-gun positions could just keep spraying 'em and killing 'em, and they'd just keep coming. . . . If somebody got killed, they just rolled him off into the barbed wire and kept coming. The machine guns would get so hot that they'd misfire or blow up.

You would defend and defend, and they'd just keep coming. They'd go through your first barrier and through your trench barrier, and they'd come up the wall. They used ladders and ropes to scale it. The walls were clay, with big bamboo spikes on 'em, so when these guys got to the top they had a spike to climb over. But they'd come over, and there would be so many of them that at some point, even if you were told to fight to the last man, you'd try to bug out. . . .

Later on in the war, I visited some posts after they'd been taken. The Viet Minh never stayed around. They would take all the weapons, destroy everything else, and by ten o'clock in the morning, by the time anybody could get there by road or plane or helicopter, the place would be completely deserted. All you'd see was a bunch of bodies. Nobody alive. . . . They'd leave their flag flying. They always took away their own bodies. You never saw a Viet Minh body, even if they suffered tremendous casualties.

> —Howard Sochurek, a former Life magazine photographer, interviewed about his experiences in the French Indochina War, in Harry Maurer, Strange Ground: Americans in Vietnam, 1945–1975, An Oral History (1989).

Six years ago this summer America stood at what Churchill described as "the highest pinnacle of her power and fame.". . . What do we find in the summer of 1951? The writs of Moscow run to lands which, with its own, number upward of 900 millions of people—a good 40 percent of all men living. . . . How can we account for our present situation unless we believe that men high in this government are concerting to deliver us to disaster? This must be the product of a great conspiracy, a conspiracy on a scale so immense as to dwarf any previous such venture in the history of man. A conspiracy of infamy so black that, when it is finally exposed, its principles shall be forever deserving of the maledictions of all honest men. . . . The American who has never known defeat in war does not expect to be again sold down the river in Asia . . . He is fighting tonight, fighting gloriously in a war on a distant American frontier made inglorious by the men he can no longer trust at the head of our affairs.

—*Senator Joe McCarthy, speech to the U.S. Senate, June 14, 1951.*

[In] this century, within the next decades, will be decided for generations whether all mankind is to become Communist, whether the whole world is to become free, or whether, in the struggle, civilization as we know it is to be completely destroyed or completely changed. It is our fate to live upon that turning point in history.

—*Whittaker Chambers, Witness, 1952.*

Let us turn now to another area of the world—Indochina. And many of you ask this question: Why is the United States spending hundreds of millions of dollars supporting the forces of the French Union in the fight against Communism in Indochina? I think perhaps if we go over to the map here, I can indicate to you why it is so vitally important. Here is Indochina. If Indochina falls, Thailand is put in an almost impossible position. The same is true of Malaya with its rubber and tin. The same is true of Indonesia. If this whole part of Southeast Asia goes under Communist domination or Communist influence, Japan, who trades and must trade with this area in order to exist, must inevitably be oriented toward the Communist regime. That

. . . **May 20, 1953.** General Henri Navarre assumes command of French forces in Indochina, announcing, "Now we can see [victory] clearly, like light at the end of the tunnel" . . . .

indicates to you and to all of us why it is vitally important that Indochina not go behind the Iron Curtain.

—*Televised speech by Vice President Richard Nixon, December 23, 1953.*

On March 15, 1954, on top of Hill Gabrielle overlooking the valley of Dien Bien Phu, Master Sergeant Besalem Abderrhaman of First Company, Fifth Battalion, Seventh Algerian Rifles, had spent his last ammunition and the small-boned but tough North Vietnamese regulars of Regiment 88, 308th People's Army Division, were now all around him in their green fatigues. They wore short, quilted jackets to protect them against the morning cold of the mountains, palm-leaf pith helmets covered with camouflage netting in which they had stuck leaves and branches from the surrounding foliage, rubber-soled sneakers with broad cleats, and cheap-looking, thin web belts and pouches in which they carried spare ammunition, grenades, and perhaps a fist-sized ball of cooked rice as an emergency ration.

But beyond Sergeant Abderrhaman's trench, there were perhaps 800 more of them—dead or dying, where French machine guns and artillery had mowed them down. A Communist officer . . . ordered the sergeant and his remaining squad in good French to get moving northward, across the barbed wire, to the rear of the Communist position.

"How do you want us to get across the barbed wire and the minefields?" inquired the sergeant.

"Just walk across the bodies of our men," said the officer. As

. . . **March 13, 1954.** The Viet Minh surround and attack the 15,000-man French garrison at Dienbienphu . . . .

the Algerians and Frenchmen began to pick their way across, the column came to a sudden halt before a dying Viet-Minh, as the Communist soldiers then were called. He looked up and his lips were moving.

"Get going," said the officer. "You can step on him. He has done his duty for the Democratic Republic of Viet-Nam."

—*Bernard Fall,* Viet-Nam Witness *(1966)*

Question: Mr. President, would you mind commenting on the strategic importance of Indochina to the free world? . . .

The President: . . . First of all, you have the specific value of a locality in its production of materials that the world needs.

Then you have the possibility that many human beings pass under a dictatorship that is inimical to the free world.

Finally, you have broader considerations that might follow what you would call the "falling domino" principle. You have a row of dominoes set up, you knock over the first one, and what will happen to the last one is the certainty that it will go over very quickly. So you could have a beginning of a disintegration that would have the most profound influences. . . . So, the possible consequences of the loss are just incalculable to the free world.

—*President Dwight D. Eisenhower, press conference, April 7, 1954.*

. . . **April 1954.** President Dwight Eisenhower and his advisers consider and eventually reject a plan to come to the aid of the besieged garrison at Dienbienphu with airstrikes and paratroopers. . . **April 26, 1954.** An international conference to consider the future of Indochina opens in Geneva, Switzerland. . . **May 7, 1954.** The Viet Minh capture Dienbienphu. . . **May 8, 1954.** Negotiations begin in Geneva to end the Indochina war. . . . . . .

SAIGON, Vietnam, May 8—The entire garrison of 10,000 men had been killed, wounded or captured when the fall of Dienbienphu to the Communist-led Viet-minh was completed today.

The beleaguered Dienbienphu redoubt fell at 6 o'clock last night after a grinding eight-week siege and a gallant defense battle that may enshrine its French Union garrison in the annals of modern military history.

The troops holding the cut-off Isabelle enclave three miles south of Dienbienphu were overrun about 2 A.M. after an unsuccessful break-out attempt. . . .

Both at Dienbienphu and in Isabelle the last hours of the battle were marked by the carnage of hand-to-hand fighting. The French defenders kept throwing grenades and firing machine-guns to the very end, with those who had run out of ammunition using their bayonets as waves of insurgents overran their positions.

—*Henry R. Lieberman, "Dienbienphu's Entire Garrison Lost,"* New York Times, *May 9, 1954.*

The conference recognizes that the essential purpose of the agreement relating to Vietnam is to settle military questions with a view to ending hostilities and that the military demarcation line is provisional and should not in any way be interpreted as constituting a political or territorial boundary. . . .

. . . **June 1, 1954.** USAF Colonel Edward G. Lansdale arrives in Saigon to command the Saigon Military Mission (SMM), which will conduct covert operations and propaganda mission in Vietnam. . . **July 20–21, 1954.** A cease-fire officially ends the first Indochina War; the Geneva Accords provide for the temporary partition of Vietnam along the 17th parallel, with the Viet Minh in power in the north and a non-Communist government headed by Emperor Bao Dai and prime minister Ngo Dinh Diem in the south; nationwide elections designed to reunify the country under one government are scheduled for July 1956 . . . . . .

... In order to ensure that sufficient progress in the restoration of peace has been made, and that all the necessary conditions obtain for free expression of the national will, general elections shall be held in July 1956 under the supervision of an international commission. ...

—*Final Declaration of the Geneva Conference, July 21, 1954.*

The Saigon Military Mission (SMM) was born in a Washington policy meeting early in 1954, when Dien Bien Phu was still holding out against the encircling Vietminh. The SMM was to enter into Vietnam quietly and assist the Vietnamese, rather than the French, in unconventional warfare.... The broad mission for the team was to undertake paramilitary operations against the enemy and to wage political-psychological warfare....

Hanoi was evacuated on 9 October [1954]. The northern SMM team left with the last French troops, disturbed by what they had seen of the grim efficiency of the Vietminh in their takeover, the contrast between the silent march of the victorious Vietminh troops in their tennis shoes and the clanking armor of the well-equipped French whose Western tactics and equipment had failed against the Communist military-political-economic campaign.

The northern team had spent the last days of Hanoi in contaminating the oil supply of the bus company for a gradual wreckage of engines in the buses, in taking the first actions for delayed sabotage of the railroad (which required teamwork with a CIA special technical team in Japan who performed

---

... **August–November 1954.** The United States begins providing military and economic assistance to the Diem regime; U.S. aircraft and ships carry refugees from North to South Vietnam. . . . .

their part brilliantly), and in writing detailed notes of potential targets for future paramilitary operations . . . The team had a bad moment when contaminating the oil. They had to work quickly at night, in an enclosed storage room. Fumes from the contaminant came close to knocking them out. Dizzy and weak-kneed, they masked their faces with handkerchiefs and completed the job.

—Lansdale Team's report on covert Saigon Military Mission in 1954 and 1955. (Col. Edward Lansdale headed a CIA team station in Saigon.)

We did not sign the Geneva Agreements. We are not bound in any way by these Agreements, signed against the will of the Vietnamese people. Our policy is a policy of peace, but nothing will lead us astray from our goal: the unity of our country—a unity in freedom and not in slavery.

—Broadcast declaration by Ngo Dinh Diem, July 16, 1955.

I have never talked or corresponded with a person knowledge-able in Indochinese affairs who did not agree that had elections been held at the time of the fighting [1954], possibly 80 per cent of the population would have voted for the Communist Ho Chi Minh as their leader rather than Chief of State Bao Dai.

—Dwight D. Eisenhower, Mandate for Change, 1963.

. . . **July 6, 1955.** Diem declares that South Vietnam is not bound by the provisions of the Geneva Accords, including the planned nationwide election in 1956. . . **October 26, 1955.** After securing a suspicious 98.2 percent majority in a national referendum affirming his role as chief of state, Diem proclaims the establishment of the Republic of South Vietnam, in which he holds the posts of president, prime minister, defense minister, and supreme commander of the armed forces; the Republic of South Vietnam is immediately recognized by the United States. . . . .

"You and your like are trying to make a war with the help of people who just aren't interested."

"They don't want Communism."

"They want enough rice," I said. "They don't want to be shot at. They want one day to be much the same as another. They don't want our white skins around telling them what they want."

"If Indochina goes . . ."

"I know that record. Siam goes. Malaya goes. Indonesia goes. What does 'go' mean? If I believed in your God and another life, I'd bet my future harp against your golden crown that in five hundred years there may be no New York or London, but they'll be growing paddy in these fields, they'll be carrying their produce to market on long poles wearing their pointed hats. The small boys will be sitting on the buffaloes. I like the buffaloes, they don't like our smell, the smell of Europeans. And remember—from a buffalo's point of view you are a European too."

"They'll be forced to believe what they are told, they won't be allowed to think for themselves."

"Thought's a luxury. Do you think the peasant sits and thinks of God and Democracy when he gets inside his mud hut at night?"

—*Graham Greene*, The Quiet American, *1955.*

The French sent Ho Chi Minh into exile but on December 19, 1946, his forces started a war for independence—started it by disemboweling more than 1000 native women in Hanoi because they had been working for, married to, or living with the French. . . . The rice-paddy-worker knew only that the underground hero and his soldiers, many of them from their own villages, were fighting and often defeating the French. To him this was "Viet Minh Nationalism." He did not know he was placing himself in the bondage of Communism; he only wanted to be free of the yoke of colonialism. . . . By the time the complex struggle came to a head at Dien Bien Phu, the free world no longer had any illusions. It was aware that the life-and-death interests of Washington and London were at stake on one side as surely as those of Moscow and Peiping were on the other.

> —*Thomas A. Dooley, M.D.*, Deliver Us From Evil: The Story of Viet Nam's Flight to Freedom *(1956).*

Our idea in Vietnam was: This is a new nation being born. It has to be something. And naturally, we Americans were convinced that the "something" should be our system of representative government, the best in the world. Furthermore, we were the guys who were there. We had the sense of mission. We were the nation that had won World War II and was honored throughout the world. . . . And Vietnam was an ideal place. It was enormously attractive in those days . . . There was a sense of a young country, which was very inspiring. It was a small country, which meant you could identify with it as a project. There was a very graceful, traditional culture, an enormously pleasant way of life. Saigon was an elegant city. The beautiful tropical foliage, the flamboyant trees, the cabarets, the lovely slim women in their gorgeous ao dais. The whole thing was just

. . . **January 11, 1956.** Diem government launches a campaign against former Viet Minh supporters in the south, arresting and imprisoning thousands; sporadic and localized armed resistance begins in the countryside. . . . .

elegant and romantic as hell. It was a dream country if you left it alone. Very seductive.

> —*Ogden Williams, quoted in Harry Maurer,* Strange Ground: Americans in Vietnam, 1945–1975, An Oral History. *[Williams first came to Vietnam as a CIA agent in 1956, when he worked for Edward Lansdale.]*

Ngo Dinh Diem is respected in Vietnam today for the miracles he has wrought. Order has replaced chaos. Communism is being defeated. A pattern of leadership which could provide an alternative to neutralism in southeast Asia is being shaped and tested. . . . Diem would be the last to deny that the U.S. has contributed a lot to his success. American aid to Vietnam, in all forms, comes to around $400 million a year. The U.S. is paying 75% of Vietnam's public costs, largely supporting its army of 150,000 men . . . Public confidence in the authority of Diem's government is all but complete—which is to say, most people perceive that it is safer to be for the national government than against it. A corresponding confidence in its purposes, and in Diem as its leader has yet to be won, but it is in the making. . . .

> —*John Osborne, "The Tough Miracle Man of Vietnam,"* Life *magazine, May 13, 1957.*

In 1946 when Chiang Kai-shek launched his attacks against us, many of our comrades and people throughout the country were very much worried: Could the war be won? I myself was also worried about this. But of one thing we were confident. At that time an American journalist named Anna Louise Strong came to Yenan. We discussed many questions in our talks, including Chiang Kai-shek, Hitler, Japan, the United States, the atom bomb, etc. I said that all the reputedly powerful reactionaries were merely paper tigers. The reason was that they were divorced from the people. You see, wasn't Hitler a paper tiger? Wasn't Hitler overthrown? I also said that the tsar was a paper tiger, the Chinese emperor was a paper tiger, Japanese imperialism was a paper tiger. You see they were all down and out. U.S. imperialism has not yet fallen and it has the atom bomb. I believe it will also fall. It is also a paper tiger . . .

—*Mao Zedong, speech in Moscow, November 18, 1957.*

My own theory about Communism is that it is master-minded by Satan . . . I think there is no other explanation for the tremendous gains of Communism in which they seem to outwit us at every turn, unless they have supernatural power and wisdom and intelligence given to them.

—*Reverend Billy Graham, 1957.*

BIENHOA, Vietnam, July 9—Increasing Communist terrorism in South Vietnam was emphasized sharply here last night when two United States soldiers, a major and a master sergeant, were

. . . **1957–59.** North Vietnam's leaders order infiltration of southern-born Communist cadres into South Vietnam along "Ho Chi Minh Trail" to direct armed insurgency against the Diem government. . . **July 8, 1959.** Two American soldiers are killed in a guerrilla attack on MAAG compound in Bienhoa, becoming the first Americans killed in the Vietnam War . . . .

killed and a captain was wounded by the Vietminh . . . According to diplomatic sources, this was the first time the Communist Vietminh has carried out a successful assassination mission against Americans.

—*"Two U.S. Soldiers Slain in Vietnam,"* New York Times, *July 10, 1959.*

PRESIDENTIAL ELECTION, 1960:

Candidate	Party	% of Popular Vote
John F. Kennedy	Democratic	49.7
Richard M. Nixon	Republican	49.5

DECEMBER 31, 1960:

U.S. Troop Level in South Vietnam—900
Total U.S. Killed in Vietnam War—8

. . . **1959–1961.** Communists launch a campaign of assassinations of local Diem government officials, killing 4,000 in 1961 alone. . . **November 8, 1960.** John F. Kennedy defeats Richard Nixon for presidency. . . **December 20, 1960.** Establishment of National Liberation Front (NLF), called by its opponents the "Viet Cong" . . . .

2

PRESIDENT JOHN F. KENNEDY came into office in 1961 promising that Americans would "pay any price" and "bear any burden" necessary to defend freedom around the globe. Inheriting a commitment to preserving an independent South Vietnam, Kennedy dramatically stepped up the level of American military involvement in that country. American policymakers believed that "counter-insurgency" techniques were the antidote to the Communists' "national liberation wars." A limited number of American military advisers, armed with the latest in American military technology, were expected to train and inspire the Army of the Republic of Vietnam (ARVN) to triumph over the ragtag forces of the Communist Viet Cong guerrillas. [The term "Viet Cong" was a derogatory phrase meaning "Vietnamese Communist" introduced by the Diem government to describe what the communists preferred to call the "National Liberation Front."] But the poorly led and poorly motivated South Vietnamese soldiers proved no match for the Viet Cong. Increasingly, American military advisers found themselves drawn into direct combat roles in 1961–63. As American casualties mounted, so did the sense of American commitment to South Vietnam. At the same time, the brutal and inefficient Diem regime stumbled from one political crisis to another. The United States offered covert assurances of support to dissatisfied South Vietnamese generals who plotted to overthrow the Diem regime. The plotters struck in early November 1963, killing Diem. Three weeks later John Kennedy himself was murdered in Dallas.

KENNEDY'S WAR, 1961–1963

JANUARY 1961

It all began in the cold.

It had been cold all week in Washington. Then early Thursday afternoon the snow came. The winds blew in icy, stinging gusts and whipped the snow down the frigid streets. Washingtonians do not know how to drive in the snow: they slide and skid and spin their wheels and panic. By six o'clock traffic had stopped all over town. People abandoned their cars in snowdrifts and marched grimly into the gale, heads down, newspapers wrapped around their necks and stuffed under coats. And still the snow fell and the winds blew.

At eight o'clock the young President-elect and his wife went to the Inaugural Concert at Constitution Hall. An hour later they left at the intermission to go on to the Inaugural Gala at the Armory. The limousine made its careful way through the blinding snow down the Mall. Bonfires had been lit along the path in a vain effort to keep the avenue clear. Great floodlights around the Washington Monument glittered through the white storm. It was a scene of eerie beauty. As stranded motorists cheered the presidential car, the President-elect told his friend William Walton, "Turn on the lights so they can see Jackie." With the light on inside the car, he settled back to read Jefferson's First Inaugural, which had been printed in the concert program. When he finished, he shook his head and said wryly, "Better than mine."

—*Arthur Schlesinger, Jr.,* A Thousand Days *(1965)*

At this point, President Eisenhower said with considerable emotion that Laos was the key to the entire area of Southeast Asia. He said that if we permitted Laos to fall, then we would have to write off all the area. . . . As he concluded these remarks, President Eisenhower stated that it was imperative that Laos be defended. He said that the United States should accept this task with our allies, if we could persuade them, and alone if we could not. He added that "our unilateral intervention would be our last desperate hope" in the event we were unable to prevail upon the other [Southeast Asia Treaty Organization] signatories to join us. . . . President-elect Kennedy commented upon the seriousness of the situation in Laos and in Southeast Asia and asked if the situation seemed to be approaching a climax. General Eisenhower stated that the entire proceeding was extremely confused but that it was clear that this country was obligated to support the existing government in Laos.

—*Memorandum of Conference on the meeting between President Eisenhower and President-elect Kennedy on Laos, January 19, 1961.*

January 21, 1961. John F. Kennedy inaugurated as President of the United States . . . .

We shall pay any price, bear any burden, meet any hardship, support any friend, oppose any foe to assure the survival and the success of liberty.

—*President John F. Kennedy, Inaugural Address, January 20, 1961.*

The President directs full examination by the Defense Department . . . of the size and composition of forces which would be desirable in the case of a possible commitment of U.S. forces to Vietnam.

—*National Security Action Memorandum 52, May 11, 1961.*

Asian leaders—at this time—do not want American troops involved in Southeast Asia other than on training missions. American combat troop involvement is not only not required, it is not desirable. Possibly Americans fail to appreciate fully the subtlety that recently colonial peoples would not look with favor upon governments which invited or accepted the return this soon of Western troops. To the extent that fear of ground troop involvement dominates our political responses to Asia in Congress or elsewhere, it seems most desirable to me to allay those paralyzing fears in confidence, on the strength of the individual statements made by leaders consulted on this trip.

. . . **April 1, 1961.** Walt Rostow, White House adviser, proposes increased U.S. military aid to South Vietnam. . . **May 11, 1961.** President Kennedy approves sending 500 additional U.S. Special Forces troops and military advisers to South Vietnam, and covert operations against North Vietnam. . . **May 9–15, 1961.** Vice President Lyndon Johnson tours Southeast Asia, meeting with Diem in South Vietnam and labeling him the "Churchill of Asia". . . **May 23, 1961.** Vice President Johnson meets with President Kennedy, urging increased U.S. aid to South Vietnam . . . .

This does not minimize or disregard the probability that open attack would bring calls for U.S. combat troops. But the present probability of open attack seems scant, and we might gain much needed flexibility in our policies if the spectre of combat troop commitment could be lessened domestically.

> —*Vice President Lyndon B. Johnson's report to President John F. Kennedy, May 23, 1961, following Johnson's diplomatic tour of Southeast Asia.*

In reference to my letter dated 15 May 1961 and in reply to the invitation that was made to me in your name by Vice President Johnson, I have the honor to send you a study of our needs to meet the new situation.

As I expressed verbally to your eminent representative, it pertains to a situation which has become very much more perilous following the events in Laos . . . It is apparent that one of the major obstacles to the Communist expansion in this area of the globe is Free Vietnam because with your firm support, we are resolved to oppose it with all our energies. Consequently, now and henceforth, we constitute the first target for the Communists to overthrow at any cost. The enormous accumulation of Russian war matériel in North Vietnam is aimed, in the judgment of foreign observers, more at South Vietnam than at Laos. We clearly realize this dangerous situation but I want to reiterate to you here, in my personal name and in the name of the entire Vietnamese people, our indomitable will to win. . . . I am convinced that with your support and so generously aided by your great, friendly nation, I will manage to reestablish law and order in our provinces, in our villages, to accelerate progress in all other areas for the edification of a society of free men, happy and prosperous. Vietnam thus constitutes a pole of attraction for the countries of Southeast Asia, for those who fight communism as well as for those who still doubt the future of the free world.

I wish to assure you, Mr. President, of the sincerity of my sentiments and most cordial wishes.

—Letter from South Vietnam President Ngo Dinh Diem to President John F. Kennedy, June 9, 1961.

For what one man's feel is worth, mine—based on very close touch with Indochina in the 1954 war and civil war afterwards till Diem took hold—is that it *is* really now or never if we are to arrest the gains made by the Viet Cong. . . . An early and hard-hitting operation has a good chance (70% would be my guess) of *arresting* things and giving Diem a chance to do better and clean up. Even if we follow up hard . . . however, the chances are not much better that we will in fact be able to *clean up* the situation. It *all* depends on Diem's effectiveness, which is very problematical. The 30% chance is that we wind up like the French in 1954; white men can't win this kind of fight.

On a 70–30 basis, I would myself favor going in.

—Memorandum from Acting Assistant Secretary of Defense William P. Bundy to Robert McNamara, October 10, 1961.

As an area for the operation of U.S. troops, SVN is not an excessively difficult or unpleasant place to operate. While the border areas are rugged and heavily forested, the terrain is comparable to parts of Korea where U.S. troops learned to live and work without too much effort . . . In the High Plateau and in the coastal plain where U.S. troops would probably be stationed, these jungle-forest conditions do not exist to any great extent. The most unpleasant feature in the coastal areas would be the heat and, in the Delta, the mud left behind by the flood. . . . The risks of backing into a major Asia war by way of SVN are present but not impressive.

> —*Cablegram from General Maxwell Taylor to President Kennedy, November 1, 1961.*

The basic issue framed by the Taylor Report is whether the U.S. shall:

a. Commit itself to the clear objective of preventing the fall of South Vietnam to Communism, and
b. Support this commitment by necessary immediate military actions and preparations for possible later actions.

The Joint Chiefs, Mr. Gilpatric, and I have reached the following conclusions:

1. The fall of South Vietnam to Communism would lead to the fairly rapid extension of Communist control . . . in the rest of mainland Southeast Asia and in Indonesia. The strategic implications worldwide . . . would be extremely serious.
2. The chances are against . . . preventing that fall by any measures short of the introduction of U.S. forces on a substantial scale. . . .
3. The introduction of a U.S. force of the magnitude of an initial 8,000 men in a flood relief context will be of great help to Diem. However, it will not convince the other side . . . that we mean business. . . .

. . . **November 3, 1961.** General Maxwell Taylor, military adviser to President Kennedy, reports to Kennedy on his recent trip to South Vietnam; he recommends increased military aid, including the dispatch of 8,000 U.S. troops under the guise of a "flood control" operation. . . . .

4. The other side can be convinced we mean business only if we accompany the initial force introduction by a clear commitment to the full objective stated above, accompanied by a warning through some channel to Hanoi that continued support of the Viet Cong will lead to punitive retaliation against North Vietnam.

5. If we act in this way, the ultimate possible extent of our military commitment must be faced. The struggle may be prolonged and Hanoi and Peiping may intervene overtly. In view of the logistic difficulties faced by the other side, I believe we can assume that the maximum U.S. forces required on the ground in Southeast Asia will not exceed 6 divisions, or about 205,000 men . . .

6. To accept the stated objective is of course a most serious decision. Military force is not the only element of what must be a most carefully coordinated set of actions. Success will depend on factors many of which are not within our control—notably the conduct of Diem himself . . . The domestic political implications of accepting the objective are also grave, although it is our feeling that the country will respond better to a firm initial position than to courses of action that lead us in only gradually, and that in the meantime are sure to involve casualties. . . .

7. In sum:

   a. We do not believe major units of U.S. forces should be introduced in South Vietnam unless we are willing to make an affirmative decision on the issue stated at the start of this memorandum.

   b. We are inclined to recommend that we do commit the U.S. to the clear objective of preventing the fall of South Vietnam to Communism and that we support this commitment by the necessary military actions.

c. If such a commitment is agreed upon, we support the recommendations of General Taylor as the first steps toward its fulfillment.

—*Memorandum to President Kennedy from Secretary of Defense Robert McNamara, November 8, 1961.*

The troops will march in; the bands will play; the crowd will cheer; and in four days everyone will have forgotten. Then we will be told we have to send in more troops. It's like taking a drink. The effect wears off, and you have to take another.

—*President John F. Kennedy to White House aide Arthur Schlesinger, Jr., November 1961.*

The deteriorating situation in South Viet-Nam requires attention to the nature and scope of United States national interests in that country. The loss of South Viet-Nam to Communism would involve the transfer of a nation of 20 million people from the free world to the Communist bloc. The loss of South Vietnam would make pointless any further discussion about the importance of Southeast Asia to the free world; we would have to face the near certainty that the remainder of Southeast Asia and Indonesia would move to a complete accommodation with Communism, if not formal incorporation with the Communist bloc . . . Further, loss of South Viet-Nam would stimulate bitter domestic controversies in the United States and would be seized upon by extreme elements to divide the country and harass the Administration. . . .

—*Rusk-McNamara Report to Kennedy, November 11, 1961.*

DECEMBER 31, 1961:

U.S. Troop Level in South Vietnam—3,200
Total U.S. Killed in Vietnam War—24

"This is a grubby, dirty method of fighting," said the plump, 45-year-old American colonel in mud-caked fatigues. Military adviser to a South Vietnamese infantry regiment, he had just returned to Saigon last week after twelve exhausting days of tramping through the Annam mountains in search of Viet Cong (Communist) guerrillas. In a slow Alabama drawl, the former paratrooper (whose name was withheld for security reasons) added ruefully: "If we could corner all the Viet Cong operating on the highland on open ground we could lay them flat in 25 minutes. But it takes weeks to find even 50 of them."

Along with the colonel, some 2,000 other American military advisers, technicians, and specialists were moving last week into the guerrilla-infested mountains of South Vietnam. Some were operating radio installations. Others were teaching road-building or showing the South Vietnamese, among them many women, how to shoot. Some would soon be piloting U.S. helicopters into areas threatened by the Communists, airlifting supplies and equipment.

Technically, the American buildup in Vietnam may be in violation of the 1954 Geneva Treaty limitations on "foreign forces" in Vietnam. But the U.S., though it accepted the treaty, did not actually sign it; moreover, the International Control

... **December 11, 1961.** First U.S. helicopter units arrive in South Vietnam... **December 14, 1961.** U.S. aircraft are authorized to fly combat missions in South Vietnam, provided a Vietnamese crew member is aboard . . . .

Commission set up to enforce the agreement, has done nothing to stop the infiltration of agents and troops from Communist North Vietnam. With more than 17,000 Communist guerrillas reported to be in action in South Vietnam, the U.S. felt it no longer could be bound by the Geneva accord. Hence Mr. Kennedy's decision to act unilaterally, and step up military aid to President Ngo Dinh Diem.

—*"Southeast Asia: The Anti-Guerrillas,"* Newsweek, *January 1, 1962.*

Technically we were advisers. Our job was to haul supplies in and out of outposts; evacuate wounded; and carry ARVN on heliborne operations. We weren't supposed to participate in the fighting. But when we started taking on fire, we knew we had to be ready to protect ourselves, and we started arming our choppers . . . At first, the VC were frightened by the choppers, but word must have gotten around quickly how vulnerable the machines were. We couldn't armor plate because the weight would lower our payload. There's so many cables and hoses running to the rotor gear box, a rifle slug could knock us out of action. Lose hydraulic oil or lubricating oil, temperatures went up and we'd have to sit down quickly. So, as our tour continued, instead of running, the VC stayed and fired back . . . As the heat increased, the problem of when and where to fire back became acute. The hawks in the squadron wanted to shoot, any chance they got. . . . Yep, we went in like boy scouts and came out like Hell's Angels.

—*Marine Lieutenant Kenneth Babbs, quoted in John Clark Pratt,* Vietnam Voices: Perspectives on the War Years, 1941–1982 *(1984).*

. . . **January 12, 1962.** "Operation Ranch Hand" is launched; USAF drops herbicides to "defoliate" enemy territory. . . **January 27, 1962.** Joint Chiefs of Staff recommend to President Kennedy that U.S. forces be deployed in Vietnam. . . **February 4, 1962.** Viet Cong shoot down a U.S. helicopter for the first time in the war . . . .

Airmobility, dig it, you weren't going anywhere. It made you feel safe, it made you feel Omni, but it was only a stunt, technology. Mobility was just mobility, it saved lives or took them all the time (saved mine I don't know how many times, maybe dozens, maybe none), what you really needed was a flexibility far greater than anything the technology could provide. . . .

—*Michael Herr,* Dispatches *(1978).*

Nothing could look more peaceful than the ripening rice paddies that rippled out in greenish-brown billows to the horizon. Driving through them on a gravel road, dotted here and there with black mounds of buffalo dung, the American Army truck driver could see only a few silent Vietnamese peasants scraping their midday bowls of rice.

Suddenly the roar of a land mine exploded under the American's radio-detection truck, hurling it 30 yards into a ditch. The American and nine Vietnamese soldiers climbed out of the truck with their rifles ready. From the once-peaceful rice paddies, some twenty Communist guerrillas swept the road with automatic gunfire. When the massacre was over, the ten lay dead. When they were found, their wounds were covered with flies, their weapons and electronic equipment gone. Among them was the American T/Sgt. James T. Davis.

Sergeant Davis, a Tennessean, was the first American to be killed by Communist guerrillas in Vietnam. Three more Americans died last week when their C-123 transport crashed in the

... **February 6, 1962.** U.S. Military Assistance Command Vietnam (MACV) is formed under command of General Paul Harkins, to oversee stepped-up U.S. military assistance, including use of American advisers to the Army of the Republic of Vietnam (ARVN). . . . .

jungle. All told, the two-year-old war these Americans were helping to fight is claiming more than 1,000 lives a month.

With the waning of the Algerian war, the war in Vietnam is the biggest in the world. It threatens to bring all Southeast Asia under Communist rule, and it could easily bring the U.S. into a direct collision with the Red Chinese. Each week, more American troops, technically known as "advisers" are committed to the former French colony of Vietnam. And steadily the fighting grows fiercer.

— *"Guerrilla Warfare,"* Newsweek, February 12, 1962.

Responding to criticism, President Kennedy said today he was being as frank as possible about United States involvement in the war in Vietnam. He asked that such sensitive matters be left to "responsible leaders" of both parties.

The President countered charges of excessive secrecy with a statement that no American combat troops "in the generally understood sense of the word" had yet been sent into Vietnam.

— *"Kennedy Denies Secrecy on Vietnam is Excessive,"* New York Times, February 15, 1962.

"There are two air forces in South Viet Nam," said an official in Saigon, "the Vietnamese and the U.S." Since the U.S. role, technically, is to instruct government pilots, Vietnamese trainees accompany the American pilots on bombing and strafing missions against the Communist Viet Cong. When fast action is needed, it is the U.S. air power that does the job. Last week that help was badly needed.

The usual method of the 25,000 Communist Viet Cong guerrillas is to attack in small numbers at scattered points, ambushing a government patrol or raiding a village. Recently, in an abrupt change of pace and tactics, the guerrillas began striking in larger numbers and concentrating their attack in the country's heavily populated southern part. The Viet Cong poured more than 200 men into a single battle, launched five other forays in batallion strength that seemed to signal the start of a spring offensive. Said one U.S. colonel: "The Viet Cong is entering a new phase of the war."

The heaviest fighting took place last week at the village of Bo Tuc, 82 miles northwest of Saigon in Tayninh province, six miles from the Cambodian border. Promptly at midnight, at the sound of five thumps on a bamboo drum, hundreds of Viet Cong guerrillas stormed from the tall grass, quickly over-ran two outposts manned by four civil guards. Their main objective was a large defense post in the center of the village occupied by 78 guards and militiamen. Racing toward the fort, protected by barbed wire and an embankment bristling with bamboo spikes, the Communists burned the surrounding huts.

The flames proved their undoing. They lost their protective cover, became silhouetted targets . . . The battle raged until morning, when three waves of government planes, some piloted by Vietnamese and some by Americans accompanied by Vietnamese trainees, finally appeared to bomb and strafe the fleeing Viet Cong. . . .

Two days later the Vietnamese went on the offensive. Flying from Saigon before dawn, 16 U.S. Army helicopters picked up a Vietnamese battalion. Their orders: to surprise 200 guerrillas that intelligence reports had located in the village of Cai Ngai, a Communist stronghold on the southeast tip of Viet Nam. Already in the area, concentrated in the Mekong Delta, were 1,500 government troops searching for the enemy in the mangrove swamps and inlets along the South China Sea.

Flying six to ten feet above the ground to hide from Communist spotters, the helicopters soon touched down near the village as AD-6 Skyraiders strafed the ground to cut off the Viet Cong retreat. But instead of racing to the village from where the startled Communists had fled (leaving behind their dinner), the Vietnamese paused under the coconut trees. "Let's move the thing forward," yelled a frustrated U.S. adviser. When the troops reached the group of huts, the main force of the Viet Cong had fled . . . Strafing had killed about 25 guerrillas. The only Vietnamese casualty was a soldier who was accidentally shot in the foot by a comrade. Six helicopters were riddled with bullets, but all returned safely. Said one U.S. pilot dryly: "They got hold of an American training manual that explains how to shoot at aircraft."

—"South Viet Nam: The Test to Come," Time magazine, March 16, 1962.

SAIGON, Vietnam, May 11—United States aid to South Vietnam has reached a peak and will start to level off, Robert S. McNamara, Defense Secretary, disclosed today.

Before departing for Washington, Mr. McNamara said he doubted whether United States military personnel assigned to South Vietnam would be increased above the present levels of strength.

There are more than 6,000 American servicemen advising,

. . . **April 9, 1962.** Two U.S. soldiers are killed in Viet Cong ambush. . . **April 15, 1962.** First U.S. Marine air units arrive in South Vietnam. . . **May 11, 1962.** U.S. Secretary of Defense Robert McNamara visits South Vietnam and meets Diem, declaring that "every quantitative measurement . . . shows that we are winning the war" . . . .

training and supporting South Vietnamese forces against the Communist guerrillas. An additional 1,000 or more American service men are believed to be either en route or destined for shipment. . . .

After 48 hours in South Vietnam Mr. McNamara was tremendously encouraged by developments. . . . "I found nothing but progress and hope for the future," he said.

> —*Homer Bigart, "M'Namara Terms Saigon Aid Ample," New York Times, May 12, 1962.*

Peasants from the village of An Dinh were gathering reeds beside a stream in the rugged mounts of Central Vietnam one day last week when they noticed two strange-looking men approaching. They were tall and fair, and wore baggy blue suits. The two men dropped to their hands and knees, and avidly scooped up water from the stream. Then they asked directions to the coastal town of Da Nang.

The men were Americans—Sgt. 1/C Francis Quinn of Niagara Falls, N.Y., and Sgt. George E. Groom of St. Joseph, Mo. Twenty-two days previously, they had been captured in a Viet Cong attack and held prisoner on a mountaintop only 5 miles away. . . .

"The rebel commander had fierce eyes," said Groom. "He insisted that 'here, everybody is equal.'

"In some ways they were. All wore ragged uniforms, no two of them alike. Some had short pants, others were in black peasant clothes."

Both Americans stressed that they had not been tortured. "We were served food twice or three times a day," said Quinn. "It was two small bowls of cold rice each time, with a bit of sun-dried fish thrown in. They made coffee out of roasted rice and gave us some hand-rolled cigarettes. Once we got permission to bathe at a trickle of water dripping from a bamboo pipe. They handed us a tiny piece of soap and warned us to use it sparingly as others needed it.

... "The guerrillas' main concern," said Sergeant Quinn, "was, as they put it, to 'handle our education.' " And for a group of jungle guerrillas, the Viet Cong were remarkably, if one-sidedly, well-informed. They argued with the two Americans about "high unemployment in the U.S." and the ability of Soviet missiles to pierce the U.S.-Canadian Distant Early Warning (DEW Line) radar screen without being detected.

Why had the Viet Cong guerrillas let their captives go free?

Neither the sergeants nor U.S. authorities could give any definite explanation. The Communist Vietnam radio said the two men had "submitted a request for gracious pardon"—but the sergeants hotly denied this. More likely the Viet Cong were simply making propaganda. By releasing the Americans, they hoped to get credit for "magnanimity" and at the same time draw attention to their "victory" over U.S. troops.

—"Sergeants Two," Newsweek, May 14, 1962.

SAIGON, Vietnam, Aug. 11—Recent developments in South Vietnam have given United States officials here a little encouragement in the protracted conflict between President Ngo Dinh Diem's supporters and the Communists. So far the encouragement is qualified, however, and no one is ready to say that the war is as good as won.

On the military side, Government forces are inflicting twice as many casualties on the Vietcong (Vietnamese Communist) guerrillas as they are receiving. On the other hand, large areas of the countryside remain under the insurgent control and much of the rest is insecure.

> —*Robert Trumbull, "Glimmer of Hope Seen in Vietnam,"* New York Times, *August 12, 1962.*

WASHINGTON, Oct. 28—President Kennedy and Premier Khrushchev reached apparent agreement today on a formula to end the crisis over Cuba and to begin talks on easing tensions in other areas.

Premier Khrushchev pledged the Soviet Union to stop work on its missile sites in Cuba, to dismantle the weapons and to crate them and take them home . . .

President Kennedy, for his part, pledged the lifting of the Cuban arms blockade when the United Nations had taken the "necessary measures," and that the United States would not invade Cuba.

> —*E.W. Kenworthy, "U.S. and Soviet Reach Accord on Cuba; Kennedy Accepts Khrushchev Pledge to Remove Missiles Under U.N. Watch,"* New York Times, *October 29, 1962.*

DECEMBER 31, 1962:

U.S. Troop Level in South Vietnam—11,000
Total U.S. Killed in Vietnam War—77

HUNG MY, Vietnam, February 4—A United States Air Force helicopter company carrying Vietnamese troops routed Com-

. . . **January 2, 1963.** Battle of Ap Bac: Viet Cong hands ARVN its first major defeat . . . . .

munist forces today from this village near the southern tip of South Vietnam.

However, the maneuver failed to achieve its goal, which was to kill or capture a strong Viet Cong [Vietnamese Communist] force that had been harassing the area.

One United States helicopter was shot down and a second was hit . . . The downed craft, the first United States helicopter to be knocked out of the skies in the fighting in Vietnam, was later repaired and flown out.

—"U.S. 'Copter Crashes in Conflict in Vietnam," New York Times, February 7, 1963.

Communist military tactics have continued thus far to keep pace with the changes in technology on the American and South Vietnamese side. . . . The arrival of American helicopters in force—more than 200 were said to be operating in Viet-Nam by mid-1963—for a while diminished Communist daytime attack capabilities. However, they soon adapted to the changed conditions, which no longer permitted them to lay siege to a fortified village or post; instead, they learned to batter its defenses to pieces in one hammer blow early enough in the night to be able to crush its resistance before daybreak and to remove booty and prisoners to safe hiding places before the helicopters could be begin to operate. As the French found out in Algeria (an experience that should be studied a great deal more than it is), helicopters turned out to be very vulnerable once the adversary learned how to direct his machine-gun fire against a moving aerial target. The insurgent soon set up "heli-

. . . **February 24, 1963.** Two U.S. helicopters are shot down while airlifting ARVN troops into battle north of Saigon . . . .

copter traps" in which a fight was deliberately started for the purpose of drawing the planes to an area where several heavy machine guns lay in wait. Operations in the Quang-Ngai, Camau, and Plaine des Joncs areas in January, April, and May, 1963, in which numerous American helicopters were hit very accurately, may be the forerunner of such a situation. Also, the possession of an increasing number of field radios by the Communists soon enabled them to set up fairly effective air-raid-warning nets . . .

In the use of small-unit tactics, the Communist forces have added a few new "twists" to their earlier considerable body of knowledge in that field. Attacks are planned according to a "Five Point Field Order" known as "One Slow Action, Four Fast Ones." This is explained as follows:

SLOW and meticulous attack preparations and rehearsals;
FAST closing in with the enemy and attack;
FAST and determined destruction of enemy resistance;
FAST mopping-up of the battle area (arms, prisoners, own casualties);
FAST withdrawal to base areas.

These five points are generally well respected, especially now that American helicopters can provide support at dawn. This explains why Communist attacks in South Viet-Nam are often broken off seemingly with no reason and at a point where, with little extra effort, the objective would have been fully attained. But perhaps the extra half-hour devoted to attainment of the objective would have exposed the unit to strafing on the way back to its hideouts; the Viet-Minh frowns on this sort of "adventurism."

Mine ambushes are also a speciality of the Vietnamese Communists. In eight years of fighting, the French lost almost 500 armored vehicles (tanks, armored cars, and amphibians), of which 84 per cent blew up on mines. . . . A survey of present operations shows that the Communists continue to place heavy emphasis on mining roads, bridges, rail beds, and even open rice fields where they are likely to constitute obligatory points of passage.

—*Bernard Fall*, The Two Vietnams, *pp. 364–367 (1963).*

[W]hen I was in Hanoi, I was able to ask President Ho Chi Minh what he felt were the essential steps to halt the bloodshed and restore peace to South Viet-Nam.

"Foreign intervention must cease," replied President Ho. "The forces and the weapons of the interventionists must be withdrawn. The 1954 Geneva Agreements must be respected and U.S. pledges not to violate these agreements by force or threat of force must also be respected. An end must be put to the barbarous attempt to uproot the population and force the people of South Viet-Nam into concentration camps. A ceasefire could presumably be arranged between the Diemist forces and those of the patriotic National-Liberation Front of South Viet-Nam. Conditions must be created in which the people of South Viet-Nam can freely elect a government of their own choice. Between such a government and that of the DRV [North Vietnam] agreements could be negotiated to abolish some of the dangerous abnormalities of the present situation and to abolish the existing trade, communications and cultural barriers between North and South. But any future government of the South must engage to respect strictly the Geneva Agreements as the DRV has done, and not enter any military blocs or permit the establishment of any foreign military bases on its territories.

—*Article by Wilfred Burchett, Australian journalist, in Moscow* New Times, *May 29, 1963.*

WASHINGTON, July 11—Secretary of Defense Robert S. McNamara said today that he foresaw a "leveling off" of defense spending, but he would not, in response to questions, indicate when.

Defense outlays have risen by $10,000,000,000 to this year's anticipated peacetime record of $53,700,000,000 since the Kennedy Administration came to office in 1961. Defense appropriation requests amounted to more than half the Federal budget of $107,900,000,000 that President Kennedy presented to Congress in January. . . .

. . . Secretary McNamara observed that in the past 24 months there had been a 100 per cent increase in the number of nuclear warheads in the strategic alert force, a 60 per cent increase in the tactical nuclear forces in Western Europe, a 45 per cent increase in Army combat-ready divisions, a 30 per cent increase in tactical air squadrons, a 60 per cent increase in airlift capability, a 100 per cent increase in ship construction and conversion to modernize the fleet and a 200 per cent increase in special forces trained to cope with guerrilla warfare.

—Jack Raymond, "M'Namara Sees Leveling of Costs," New York Times, July 12, 1963.

SAIGON, Vietnam, July 31—Buddhist leaders criticized the United States Ambassador Frederick E. Nolting, Jr., today for his recent statement that he had not seen any evidence of religious persecution during his two and a half years in South Vietnam.

The Buddhists appear to believe that American officials here

... May–August 1963. Buddhist protests against Diem government, including fiery suicides by Buddhist monks in the streets . . . .

are too preoccupied with the country's leaders and know too little of the people.

A Buddhist spokesman said Mr. Nolting had never set foot in a pagoda. The embassy refused comment on this statement.

> —*"Vietnam Buddhists Criticize U.S. Envoy,"* New York Times, *August 1, 1963.*

We are launched on a course from which there is no respectable turning back: the overthrow of the Diem government. There is no turning back in part because U.S. prestige is already publicly committed to this end in large measure and will become more so as the facts leak out. In a more fundamental sense, there is no turning back because there is no possibility, in my view, that the war can be won under a Diem administration. . . . The chance of bringing off a generals' coup depends on them to some extent; but it depends at least as much on us.

> —*Cablegram from U.S. Ambassador to South Vietnam Henry Cabot Lodge to Secretary of State Dean Rusk, August 29, 1963.*

. . . Those people who say that we ought to withdraw from Vietnam are wholly wrong, because if we withdraw from Vietnam, the Communists would control Vietnam. Pretty soon Thailand, Cambodia, Laos, Malaya would go and all of Southeast Asia would be under the control of the Communists and under the domination of the Chinese.

> —*President John F. Kennedy, televised interview with Walter Cronkite, September 2, 1963.*

. . . **August 21, 1963.** Diem government attacks Buddhist temples, closes universities in Saigon and Hue. . . **August 22, 1963.** Henry Cabot Lodge become U.S. Ambassador to South Vietnam . . . .

[I have] today approved recommendation that no initiative should now be taken to give any active covert encouragement to a coup. There should, however, be urgent covert effort with closest security, under broad guidance of Ambassador to identify and build contacts with possible alternative leadership as and when it appears. Essential that this effort be totally secure and fully deniable . . .

—President John F. Kennedy, cablegram to U.S. Ambassador to South Vietnam Henry Cabot Lodge, October 5, 1963.

We are particularly concerned about hazard that an unsuccessful coup, however carefully we avoid direct engagement, will be laid at our door by public opinion almost everywhere. Therefore, while sharing your view that we should not be in position of thwarting coup, we would like to have option of judging and warning on any plan with poor prospects of success. We recognize that this is a large order, but President wants you to know of our concern.

—National Security Adviser McGeorge Bundy, cablegram to Ambassador Henry Cabot Lodge, October 25, 1963.

Diem: Some units have made a rebellion and I want to know, what is the attitude of the U.S.?

Lodge: I do not feel well enough informed to be able to tell you. I have heard the shooting, but am not acquainted with all

. . . **September 24, 1963.** Robert McNamara and General Maxwell Taylor arrive in Vietnam on fact-finding tour . . . .

the facts. Also, it is 4:30 A.M. in Washington and the U.S. Government cannot possibly have a view.

> —*Cablegram from Henry Cabot Lodge to State Department, reporting on a telephone conversation with Ngo Dinh Diem, November 1, 1963.*

DALLAS, Nov. 22—President John Fitzgerald Kennedy was shot and killed by an assassin today.

He died of a wound in the brain caused by a rifle bullet that was fired at him as he was riding through downtown Dallas in a motorcade.

Vice President Lyndon Baines Johnson, who was riding in the third car behind Mr. Kennedy's, was sworn in as the 36th President of the United States 99 minutes after Mr. Kennedy's death.

> —*Tom Wicker, "Kennedy is Killed by Sniper as He Rides in Car in Dallas; Johnson Sworn in on Plane,"* New York Times, *November 23, 1963.*

In downtown Dallas enthusiasm grew . . . The car turned off Main Street, the President happy and waving, Jacqueline erect and proud by his side, and Mrs. Connally saying, "You certainly can't say that the people of Dallas haven't given you a nice welcome," and the automobile turning on to Elm Street and down the slope past the Texas School Book Depository, and the shots, faint and frightening, suddenly distinct over the

---

roar of the motorcade, and the quizzical look on the President's face before he pitched over, and Jacqueline crying, "Oh, no, no . . . Oh, my God, they have shot my husband," and the horror, the vacancy.

—*Arthur Schlesinger, Jr.*, A Thousand Days *(1965).*

The death of President Kennedy came at a time when his Administration was seeking to shape a new foreign policy to cope with far-reaching changes in the world outlook. . . .

In Southeast Asia, Communist pressure, with the encouragement of Peking, was sustained in South Vietnam and in Laos. Despite a United States investment of about $2.5 billion in aid to the Government there and the presence of about 16,500 American troops, the Communist-led Vietcong guerrillas sustained their offensive.

The situation in the country which President Kennedy regarded as possibly the key to control of other non-Communist sections of Southeast Asia, was complicated by a political crisis.

Earlier this month, the Government of President Ngo Dinh Diem was swept out by a military coup led by generals friendly to the United States. President Diem and his brother, Ngo Dinh Nhu, regarded as the real power in the Government, were assassinated.

The Diem Government had incurred the wrath of the generals and the displeasure of the United States by a political repression of Buddhist elements in the country. Buddhist priests had committed suicide on the streets to dramatize what they insisted was the persecution of their movement by the Roman Catholic Diem family. They transformed themselves into human torches.

President Diem resisted the appeals of the Kennedy Administration to adopt a more lenient attitude toward the Buddhists. The position of the Administration was that the measures against the Buddhists had made the Diem Government so unpopular that a victory against the Communists would be unlikely unless there were political reforms.

The disappearance of the Diem regime left many questions about the future of South Vietnam unanswered. There was no certainty that the new regime would be able to unite the country and prosecute the war against the Vietcong effectively.

Communist control of South Vietnam would almost surely mean collapse of the shaky coalition regime in Laos and endanger pro-Western Thailand and the neutralist regimes in Cambodia and Burma.

> —"Death Came as Kennedy Sought to Shape a New Foreign Policy Geared to Changes in the World Outlook," New York Times, November 23, 1963.

As *Air Force One* carried us swiftly back to Washington after the tragedy in Dallas, I made a solemn private vow: I would devote every hour of every day during the remainder of John Kennedy's unfulfilled term to achieving the goals he had set. That meant seeing things through in Vietnam as well as coping with the many other international and domestic problems he had faced. I made this promise not out of blind loyalty but because I was convinced that the broad lines of his policy, in Southeast Asia and elsewhere, had been right. They were consistent with the goals the United States had been trying to accomplish in the world since 1945.

> —Lyndon B. Johnson, The Vantage Point (1971).

The President has reviewed the discussions of South Vietnam which occurred in Honolulu, and has discussed the matter further with Ambassador Lodge. He directs that the following guidance be issued to all concerned:

1. It remains the central object of the United States in South Vietnam to assist the people and Government of that country to win their contest against the externally directed and supported Communist conspiracy. . . .

4. The President expects that all senior officers of the Government will move energetically to insure the full unity of support for established U.S. policy in South Vietnam. Both in Washington and in the field, it is essential that the Government be unified. It is of particular importance that express or implied criticisms of officers of other branches be scrupulously avoided in all contacts with the Vietnamese Government and with the press. . . .

> —National Security Action Memorandum No. 273 by McGeorge Bundy, November 26, 1963.

"Present policy says that there is a war which can be won in South Viet Nam alone. It says that the war can be won at a limited expenditure of American lives and resources somewhere commensurate with our national interests in South Viet Nam.

Both assumptions may be in error. There may be no war to be won in South Viet Nam alone. There may be only a war which will, in time, involve U.S. forces throughout Southeast Asia, and finally throughout China itself in search of victory. What

. . . **November 24, 1963.** President Lyndon Johnson reaffirms U.S. support for South Vietnam. . . . .

national interests in Asia would steel the American people for the massive costs of an ever-deepening involvement of that kind? It may be that we are confronted with a dilemma not unlike that which faced us in Korea a decade ago. It will be recalled that Mr. Eisenhower's response was not to pursue the war to victory but to go to Korea to make peace, in reality, a truce.

—Memorandum from Senator Mike Mansfield to President Lyndon Johnson, December 7, 1963.

In accordance with your request this morning, this is a summary of my conclusions after my visit to Vietnam on December 19–20. . . . The situation is very disturbing. Current trends, unless reversed in the next 2–3 months, will lead to neutralization at best and more likely to a Communist-controlled state . . . We should watch the situation very carefully, running scared, hoping for the best, but preparing for more forceful moves if the situation does not show early signs of improvement.

—Memorandum from Robert McNamara to President Johnson, December 21, 1963.

December 31, 1963:

U.S. Troop Level in South Vietnam—16,500
Total U.S. Killed in Vietnam War—195

. . . **December 19, 1963.** Robert McNamara arrives in Saigon to evaluate war effort. . . . . .

3

PRESIDENT LYNDON BAINES JOHNSON transformed the Vietnam war into a major conflict. Hundreds of thousands of American combat soldiers and Marines took over from the counterinsurgency advisers of the Kennedy years. Americans began to learn a new terminology of war, including terms such as "search and destroy" and "kill ratio." Johnson launched an air war designed to bring North Vietnam to its knees at the bargaining table. The Communists in turn stepped up the level of their own infiltration of supplies and men from the North along the Ho Chi Minh Trail.

In response to alleged attacks on American destroyers by North Vietnamese PT boats, the United States Congress passed the Gulf of Tonkin Resolution in August 1964. This resolution would serve Lyndon Johnson as the functional equivalent of a formal declaration of war. However, as American casualties mounted, so too did doubts about the origins and wisdom of the American commitment in South Vietnam. Protests were heard both in the halls of Congress and, increasingly, in the streets of the United States. But through the end of 1967, only a minority of Americans could imagine the possibility that the United States would not eventually prevail over its enemies in Vietnam.

JOHNSON'S WAR, 1964–1967

[The] only realistic course of action to examine is one that would involve direct U.S. action against North Vietnam . . . [P]reliminary analysis is that the best way to start might be through a blockade of Haiphong—not because the short-term effect would be major, even in POL [Petroleum, oil, lubrication supplies], but because this is a recognized military action that hits at the sovereignty of North Vietnam and almost inevitably means we would go further.

The next steps—which we should foreshadow at the outset—would be to hit by air attack at: (a) the key rail lines to Communist China; (b) the key road nets to Laos and South Vietnam; (c) camps (which we can now identify) used for training cadres for South Vietnam; (d) key industrial com-

---

January 2, 1964. President Johnson receives report recommending expansion of covert activities against North Vietnam; known as Oplan 34A, it includes plans for naval intelligence-gathering and for raids on North Vietnamese coast that will lead to the Gulf of Tonkin incident in August. . . **January 14, 1964.** Viet Cong down a U.S. B-26 bomber . . . **January 30, 1964.** Military coup in Saigon. . . **February 1, 1964.** Oplan 34A begins covert operations. . . **February 13, 1964.** Walt Rostow sends memo to Secretary of State Dean Rusk advocating U.S. bombing of North Vietnam. . . **March 1, 1964.** Deputy Defense Secretary William Bundy sends memo to President Johnson recommending stepped-up war effort, including bombing of North Vietnam . . . .

plexes, notably the limited number of power stations and the few showcase industrial plants. We should probably make clear we do *not* intend, at least at the outset, to attack Hanoi and Haiphong except on a pinpoint basis under the above heading (d). It is not people we are after, but the will of the government and its capacity to act and to receive help in acting. . . .

The military actions proposed would normally require a declaration of war under the Constitution. But this seems a blunt instrument carrying heavy domestic overtones and above all not suited to the picture of punitive and selective action only.

The opposite alternative of no resort at all to the Congress also seems unsatisfactory. We have no armed attack as in Korea and no sudden change of events as in Cuba.

The best answer seems to be a resolution along the lines of the Offshore Islands Resolution. That resolution took several days to pass, however, and this time we have doubtful friends in key quarters on the Hill. To ask for a resolution and not act at all would give all too much time for world pressures to build up. Perhaps the best, though not a perfect, answer is to start the blockade at once, but await the resolution for other actions.

—*Draft Memorandum for President Johnson by Assistant Secretary of Defense William P. Bundy, March 1, 1964.*

Scenario for a Congressional resolution

The first necessity, if we are to have a resolution, is to prepare the case in favor. This requires that the Administration be ready

. . . **March 8–12, 1964.** Robert McNamara and General Maxwell Taylor visit South Vietnam on fact-finding mission. . . **March 17, 1964.** McNamara and Taylor report to President Johnson at meeting of National Security Council; Johnson directs that planning for bombing of North "proceed energetically". . . **May 12–13, 1964.** McNamara and Taylor visit Vietnam on fact-finding mission; returning to U.S., they call for increased aid to South Vietnam . . . . .

to give answers to a whole series of disagreeable questions. Some of the more significant questions and possible answers follow:

1. Q. Does this resolution imply a blank check for the President to go to war over Southeast Asia?

   A. The resolution will indeed permit selective use of force, but hostilities on a larger scale are not envisaged, and in any case any large escalation would require a call-up of Reserves and thus a further appeal to the Congress. More broadly, there is no intent to usurp the powers of the Congress, but rather a need for confirmation of the powers of the President as Commander in Chief in an election year . . .

   —Memorandum by William Bundy for discussion, June 10, 1964.

My fellow Americans:

As President and Commander in Chief, it is my duty to the American people to report that renewed hostile actions against United States ships on the high seas in the Gulf of Tonkin have

. . . **May 18, 1964.** President Johnson asks Congress for $125 million more in economic and military aid for South Vietnam. . . **June 2, 1964.** In a press conference, President Johnson denies the U.S. has any plans to extend war to North Vietnam. . . **June 20, 1964.** General William Westmoreland is appointed commander of MACV (Military Assistance Command Vietnam). . . **July 7, 1964.** Maxwell Taylor becomes U.S. ambassador to South Vietnam . . . **July 30–31, 1964.** South Vietnamese PT boats raid North Vietnamese islands in Tonkin Gulf as part of Oplan 34A; USS *Maddox* monitors North Vietnamese radar and radio transmissions. . . **August 2, 1964.** U.S. destroyer *Maddox* attacked by North Vietnamese PT boats in the Gulf of Tonkin. . . **August 3–4, 1964.** South Vietnamese PT boats attack installations on North Vietnamese coast. . . **August 4, 1964.** U.S. destroyers *Maddox* and *Turner Joy* report attack by North Vietnamese PT boats in the Gulf of Tonkin, although the actual circumstances of the incident are murky. . . **August 4, 1964.** U.S. warplanes launch retaliatory attacks on North Vietnam; North Vietnamese capture first U.S. POW from downed plane. . . . .

today required me to order the military forces of the United States to take action in reply.

The initial attack on the destroyer *Maddox* on Aug. 2 was repeated today by a number of hostile vessels attacking two U.S. destroyers with torpedoes. . . .

I have today met with the leaders of both parties in the Congress of the United States and I have informed them that I shall immediately request the Congress to pass a resolution making it clear that our Government is united in its determination to take all necessary measures in support of freedom and in defense of peace in Southeast Asia.

—*President Lyndon B. Johnson, televised address to the nation, August 4, 1964.*

Through the darkness, from the west and south, the intruders boldly sped. There were at least six of them, Russian-designed "Swatow" gunboats armed with 37mm and 28mm guns, and P-4s. At 9:52 they opened fire on the destroyers with automatic weapons, this time from as close as 2,000 yards.

The night glowed eerily with the nightmarish glare of air-dropped flares and boats' searchlights. For 3½ hours, the small boats attacked in pass after pass. Ten enemy torpedoes sizzled through the water. Each time the skippers, tracking the fish by radar, maneuvered to evade them. Gunfire and gun smells and shouts stung the air. Two of the enemy boats went down. Then, at 1:30 A.M., the remaining PTs ended the fight, roared off through the black night to the north.

—*"Action in Tonkin Gulf," Time magazine, August 14, 1964.*

For all I know, our Navy was shooting at whales out there.

—*President Lyndon Baines Johnson, private conversation, spring 1965.*

Whereas naval units of the Communist regime in Vietnam, in violation of the principles of the Charter of the United Nations and of international law, have deliberately and repeatedly attacked United States naval vessels lawfully present in international waters, and have thereby created a serious threat to international peace. . . . Now therefore, be it

Resolved by the Senate and House of Representatives of the United States of America in Congress assembled,

That the Congress approves and supports the determination of the President, as Commander in Chief, to take all necessary measures to repel any armed attack against the forces of the United States and to prevent further aggression. . . .

—Gulf of Tonkin Resolution, August 7, 1964.

WASHINGTON, Aug. 7—The House of Representatives and the Senate approved today the resolution requested by President Johnson to strengthen his hand in dealing with Communist aggression in Southeast Asia.

After a 40-minute debate, the House passed the resolution 416 to 0. Shortly afterward the Senate approved it, 88 to 2. Senate debate, which began yesterday afternoon, lasted nine hours. . . .

Except for Senators Wayne L. Morse, Democrat of Oregon, and Ernest Gruening, Democrat of Alaska, who cast the votes against the resolution, members in both houses uniformly praised the President for the retaliatory action he had ordered against North Vietnamese torpedo boats and their bases after the second torpedo boat attack on United States destroyers in the Gulf of Tonkin.

. . . **August 7, 1964.** U.S. Congress passes Tonkin Gulf Resolution. . . . .

There was also general agreement that Congress could not reject the President's requested resolution without giving an impression of disunity and non-support that did not, in fact, exist.

There was no support for the thesis on which Senators Morse and Gruening based their opposition—that the resolution was "unconstitutional" because it was "a predated declaration of war reserved to Congress."

> —*W.E. Kenworthy, "Congress Backs President on Southeast Asia Moves," New York Times, August 8, 1964.*

I have had advice to load our planes with bombs and to drop them on certain areas that I think would enlarge the war and escalate the war, and result in our committing a good many American boys to fighting a war that I think ought to be fought by the boys of Asia to help protect their own land.

> —*President Lyndon B. Johnson, campaign speech, August 29, 1964.*

Only hours away from the greatest Presidential plurality in history, Lyndon Johnson was solemnly cautious. He thought he could lose 12 states, and the thought pained him. "He wants to make it unanimous," a friend remarked.

> —*"The Triumphant Ticket Whoops It Up and Saddles Up Way Down at the LBJ," Life magazine, November 13, 1964.*

. . . **October 30, 1964.** 5 Americans are killed and 6 B-57 bombers destroyed in Viet Cong attack on Bienhoa Air Base. . . **November 3, 1964.** Lyndon Johnson defeats Barry Goldwater in presidential race . . . .

PRESIDENTIAL ELECTION, 1964:

Candidate	Party	% of Popular Vote
Lyndon B. Johnson	Democratic	61.1
Barry M. Goldwater	Republican	38.5

The once sleek B-57 jet fighter-bombers at the Bien Hoa air-base, 20 miles northeast of Saigon, lay blasted and burned. The wreckage was testimony to one of the worst military—and certainly the worst propaganda—setbacks suffered by the U.S. and South Vietnamese military in the long grinding war against the Communist Vietcong.

Shortly after midnight on the previous night, a band of guerrillas had lugged a half dozen 81-mm mortars to a brush-covered slope just over half a mile from the edge of the airbase. There they zeroed in on the base control tower near the enlisted men's huts and opened fire. With murderous effect the shells lobbed onto huts and the ramp where U.S. helicopters, Sky-raider attack bombers and some 30-odd B-57s stood wingtip to wingtip. The barrage lasted only half an hour. Then the guerrillas picked up their mortars and slithered off into the dark countryside.

The base was a shambles: four Americans and two Viet-namese dead, 72 Americans and five Vietnamese wounded, five B-57s worth $1.25 million each destroyed, 15 more in various states of disrepair.

While Americans back home pondered the incredible slip-up in security that could allow such a fiasco to happen, U.S. personnel on the base marveled only that it hadn't happened sooner.

"The attack didn't come as a surprise," said an Air Force

60 WITNESS TO WAR: VIETNAM

officer, "and it can happen again." He patted the U.S. pistol on his hip and said, "We're not wearing these guns to play cowboy. This is *not* a secure area."

— *"U.S. Bombers Are Blasted in Vietnam,"* Life *magazine, November 13, 1964.*

Every time I get a military recommendation, it seems to me that it calls for a large scale bombing. I have never felt that this war will be won from the air, and it seems to me that what is much more needed and would be more effective is a larger and stronger use of rangers and special forces and marines, or other appropriate military strength on the ground and on the scene. I am ready to look with great favor on that kind of increased American effort, directed at the guerrillas and aimed to stiffen the aggressiveness of Vietnamese military units up and down the line. Any recommendation that you or General Westmoreland take in this sense will have immediate attention from me, although I know that it may involve the acceptance of larger American sacrifices.

— *President Lyndon B. Johnson to Ambassador to South Vietnam Maxwell Taylor, December 1964.*

DECEMBER 31, 1964:

U.S. Troop Level in South Vietnam—23,000
Total U.S. Killed in Vietnam War—401

. . . **December 1 and 3, 1964.** White House meetings lay plans for bombing of North Vietnam. . . **December 14, 1964.** Operation Barrel Roll, secret U.S. bombing campaign in Laos, begins. . . **December 24, 1964.** 2 Americans killed in Viet Cong attack on U.S. billets in Saigon . . . .

The situation in Vietnam is deteriorating, and without new U.S. action defeat appears inevitable—probably not in a matter of weeks or perhaps even months, but within the next year or so. There is still time to turn it around, but not much . . . The policy of graduated and continuing reprisal outlined in Annex A is the more promising course available, in my judgment. . . .

Annex A—A Policy of Sustained Reprisal

. . . We believe that the best available way of increasing our chance of success in Vietnam is the development and execution of a policy of *sustained reprisal* against North Vietnam—a policy in which air and naval action against the North is justified by and related to the whole Viet Cong campaign of violence and terror in the South.

While we believe that the risks of such a policy are acceptable, we emphasize that its costs are real. It implies significant U.S. air losses even if no full air war is joined, and it seems likely that it would eventually require an extensive and costly effort against the whole air defense system of North Vietnam. U.S. casualties would be higher—and more visible to American feelings—than those sustained in the struggle in South Vietnam.

Yet measured against the costs of defeat in Vietnam, this program seems cheap. And even if it fails to turn the tide—as it may—the value of the efforts seems to us to exceed its cost.

> —*Memorandum for President Johnson from McGeorge Bundy, February 7, 1965.*

. . . **February 4, 1965.** National Security Adviser McGeorge Bundy arrives in South Vietnam to discuss political situation with Ambassador Taylor. . . **February 7, 1965.** Viet Cong attack Pleiku airbase, 8 Americans are killed; Bundy, Taylor and General Westmoreland telephone President Johnson, urging retaliatory air strikes against North Vietnam . . . .

South Vietnam is fighting for its life against a brutal campaign of terror and armed attack inspired, directed, supplied, and controlled by the Communist regime in Hanoi. This flagrant aggression has been going on for years, but recently the pace has quickened and the threat has now become active.

The war in Vietnam is a new kind of war, a fact as yet poorly understood in most parts of the world. Much of the confusion that prevails in the thinking of many people, and even many governments, stems from this basic misunderstanding. For in Vietnam a totally new brand of aggression has been loosed against an independent people who want to make their own way in peace and freedom. . . .

Above all, the war in Vietnam is *not* a spontaneous and local rebellion against the established government. . . . In Vietnam a Communist government has set out deliberately to conquer a sovereign people in a neighboring state. And to achieve its end, it has used every resource of its own government to carry out its carefully planned program of concealed aggression. North Vietnam's commitment to seize control of the South is no less total than was the commitment of the regime in North Korea in 1950. But knowing the consequences of the latter's undisguised attack, the planners in Hanoi have tried desperately to conceal their hand. They have failed and their aggression is as real as that of an invading army.

> —*U.S. State Department,* Aggression From the North: The Record of North Vietnam's Campaign to Conquer South Vietnam, *February 1965.*

The price of war in Viet Nam went up sharply last weekend: in retaliation against Communist guerrilla raids which killed eight

Americans and wounded more than 100, President Johnson ordered joint U.S. and South Vietnamese jet aircraft attacks on barracks and staging areas in the southern part of North Viet Nam. . . .

[A]t week's end came massed Communist guerrilla attacks on two large American compounds at Pleiku, a mountain town 240 miles north of Saigon, where about 1,000 American military men are stationed. When President Johnson received word of these raids, he conferred by phone with Defense, State Department and CIA officials, convened a Saturday night session of the National Security Council, made the decision to launch jet attacks on North Vietnamese staging areas. Next morning he met again with the NSC, reviewing the results of the air strikes.

The President wanted it made clear that the attacks were retaliatory in nature and did not represent a general expansion of the Vietnamese war. To that effect, Press Secretary George Reedy issued a statement: "Today's joint response was carefully limited to military areas which are supplying men and arms for attacks in South Viet Nam. As in the case of the North Vietnamese attacks in the Gulf of Tonkin last August, the response is appropriate and fitting."

—"Attacks in Retaliation," Time magazine, February 12, 1965.

On a crisp California morning last week, the huge jet transports began touching down at Travis Air Force Base outside San Francisco and discharging their somber cargoes. First came the dead, in their flag-draped, regulation coffins, and then the

. . . **February 10, 1965.** Vietcong destroy U.S. barracks at Quinhon, killing 23 Americans . . . **February 22, 1965.** General Westmoreland requests two battalions of U.S. Marines to guard Da Nang airbase. . . **February 27, 1965.** U.S. State Department releases "Aggression from the North," a "White Paper" laying out the case for U.S. policies in South Vietnam.

wounded, strapped to their litters. These were the casualties of the heaviest Communist assaults yet against American installations in South Vietnam—the men whose agonies had triggered the U.S. Government, after months and years of weighing the consequences, into sending its bombers roaring in on repeated strikes against North Vietnam.

The soldiers, living and dead, who came into Travis were also tangible evidence of a series of events almost too dizzying to absorb—events that for the first time in the three years since U.S. troops went to Vietnam in force shocked the American people into some sense of being at war. . . . With that, not only Americans but people everywhere on Earth felt the sudden chill that makes living in the second half of the twentieth century a new departure in man's experience: a chill born of the awareness that any small localized war may, through misjudgment or mischance, flare up into a holocaust that could blot out civilization.

—Newsweek, *February 22, 1965.*

SAIGON, South Vietnam, Feb. 28—The highest American and South Vietnamese officials here say they are "virtually certain" that President Johnson has decided to open a continuing, limited air war against North Vietnam to bring about a negotiated settlement of the Vietnam problem on honorable terms.

They say the air war would be unrelated to specific provocation.

—Robert Kleiman, *"U.S. Said to Plan Limited Air War As Lever on Hanoi,"* New York Times, *March 1, 1965.*

SAIGON, South Vietnam, March 2—More than 100 United States jet aircraft bombed a North Vietnamese munitions depot today and also provided air cover for 60 South Vietnamese bombers striking at a Communist naval base . . .

The missions were carried out by the largest number of planes yet used in one day against targets in North Vietnam . . .

The step-up in the war indicated by the raids was further underlined by reports that a United States Marine unit would be landed on the coast of South Vietnam later this week to provide security for the air base at Danang.

> —Jack Langguth, "160 U.S. and Saigon Planes Bomb 2 Bases in North in Record Raid; Continuing Strikes Are Expected," New York Times, March 3, 1965.

SAIGON, South Vietnam, Monday, March 8—United States Marines began landing this morning at the bay north of Danang to take up security duties around the large United States jet airfield there.

The marines, in full battle gear, met no opposition from Vietcong guerrillas in the area. South Vietnamese troops and advance marine patrols had secured the coast before the landing . . .

A cluster of Vietnamese girls, students at Central Vietnamese schools, wrapped garlands around the necks of the first marines to trot ashore from landing craft that had carried them from transport ships half a mile offshore. . . .

The marine force consists of two "battalion landing teams," or reinforced battalions, totaling more than 1,500 men apiece.

. . . **March 2, 1965.** Operation Rolling Thunder, a sustained bombing attack on North Vietnam, begins; it will continue with short interruptions until October 1968. . . **March 8, 1965.** U.S. Marines land in South Vietnam, first ground combat units assigned to the war.

They raise to 27,000 the number of American military men in South Vietnam. A thousand more Army advisers and support personnel are expected this year.

—Jack Langguth, "Marines Land to Guard Danang Base," New York Times, March 8, 1965.

WASHINGTON, March 7 (AP)—Secretary of State Dean Rusk said today that the two new battalions of marines to be stationed in South Vietnam would shoot back if shot at.

But he stressed that the marines' mission was to put a tight security ring around Danang Air Base, thus relieving South Vietnamese ground forces for combat.

— "Rusk Delineates Task of Marines," New York Times, March 8, 1965.

The main topic of conversation in Danang last week was the impending arrival of two battalions of U.S. Marines to help defend the airbase perimeter. But with the stepped-up Viet Cong offensives throughout the country, especially around Bongson and Danang, even they may not be enough to keep the strategically vital northern third of the country from falling to Communist arms. The U.S. air strikes to the North—no longer tit-for-tat but now steady, measured assaults on Viet Cong supply lines—must be backed up by success on the ground within South Viet Nam if Washington's policy is to succeed. After all, hitting the North loses its meaning if the South falls.

— "South Viet Nam: A Matter of Time?", Time magazine, March 12, 1965.

War is always attractive to young men who know nothing about it, but we had also been seduced into uniform by Kennedy's challenge to "ask what you can do for your country" and by the missionary idealism he had awakened in us. America seemed omnipotent then: the country could still claim it had never lost a war, and we believed we were ordained to play cop to the Communists' robber and spread our own political faith around the world . . . So, when we marched into the rice paddies on that damp March afternoon, we carried, along with our packs and rifles, the implicit convictions that the Viet Cong would be quickly beaten and that we were doing something altogether noble and good. We kept the packs and rifles; the convictions we lost.

> —*Philip Caputo,* A Rumor of War *(1977). [Caputo was an infantry officer with the 9th Marine Expeditionary Brigade, the first U.S. combat unit sent to Vietnam in March 1965.]*

U.S. aims:

70%—to avoid a humiliating U.S. defeat (to our reputation as a guarantor).
20%—to keep SVN (and the adjacent) territory from Chinese hands.
10%—to permit the people of SVN to enjoy a better, freer way of life.

> —*Memorandum from John T. McNaughton, Assistant Secretary of Defense, to Secretary of Defense Robert McNamara, March 24, 1965.*

. . . **March 24, 1965.** Antiwar "teach-in" held at University of Michigan; the teach-in movement will soon spread to many other American campuses . . . .

In order to rationalize, that is to sell, the wider war, we are being told by Secretary McNamara and others that this war is a decisive test for the future. It will decide the future of "wars of liberation." This is a profoundly and dangerously false notion and it shows a lamentable lack of knowledge and understanding of the revolutionary upheavals of the epoch in which we live.

It assumes that revolutionary uprisings against established authority are manufactured in Peking or in Moscow, and that they would not happen if they were not instigated, supported, and directed from one of the capitals of Communism. If this were true, the revolutionary movements could be suppressed once and for all by knocking out Peking or Moscow. They little know the Hydra who think that the Hydra has only one head and that it can be cut off.

Experience shows that there is no single central source of the revolutionary upheavals of our epoch. What is there that is common to the Irish rebellion, to the Jewish uprising in Palestine, to the civil war in Cuba, to the Arab rebellion in Algeria, to the Huk revolt in the Philippines?

What is common to them all is violent discontent with the established order and a willingness of a minority of the discontented to die in the attempt to overthrow it.

What has confused many well-meaning Americans is that in some of these rebellions, though by no means in all of them, Communists have become the leaders of the rebellion. The resistance to the Nazis in France and Italy contained a high proportion of Communists among the active partisans. But 20 years later it is General de Gaulle who presides over France.

It would be well to abandon the half-baked notion that the war in Southeast Asia will be decisive for the future of revolutionary upheavals in the world. Revolution is a homegrown product, and it could not be stamped out decisively once and for all—supposing we had such delusions of grandeur—by stamping out Red China.

In Southeast Asia we have entangled ourselves in one of the many upheavals against the old regime, and we shall not make things any better by thrashing around with ascending violence.

—*Walter Lippman*, New York Herald-Tribune, *March 31, 1965.*

On Thursday April 1, the President made the following decisions with respect to Vietnam:

. . . 5. The President approved an 18–20,000 man increase in U.S. military support forces to fill out existing units and supply needed logistic personnel.

6. The President approved the deployment of two additional Marine Battalions and one Marine Air Squadron and associated headquarters and support elements.

7. The President approved a change of mission for all Marine Battalions deployed to Vietnam to permit their more active use under conditions to be established and approved by the Secretary of Defense in consultation with the Secretary of State. . . .

11. The President desires that with respect to the actions in paragraphs 5 through 7, premature publicity be avoided by all possible precautions. The actions themselves should be taken as rapidly as practicable, but in ways that should minimize any appearance of sudden changes in policy, and official statements

. . . **April 1–2, 1965.** National Security Council meetings decide on expanded U.S. war effort in South Vietnam, with U.S. ground forces taking the offense against the Viet Cong. . . **April 6, 1965.** President Lyndon Johnson authorizes offensive operations by U.S. ground combat forces in South Vietnam . . . .

on these troop movements will be made only with the direct approval of the Secretary of Defense, in consultation with the Secretary of State. The President's desire is that these movements and changes should be understood as being gradual and wholly consistent with existing policy.

—*National Security Action Memorandum No. 328, April 6, 1965.*

Tonight Americans and Asians are dying for a world where each people may choose its own path to change.

This is the principle for which our ancestors fought in the valleys of Pennsylvania. It is the principle for which our sons fight in the jungles of Vietnam.

Vietnam is far from this quiet campus. We have no territory there, nor do we seek any. The war is dirty and brutal and difficult. And some 400 young men—born into an America bursting with opportunity and promise—have ended their lives on Vietnam's steaming soil.

Why must we take this painful road?

Why must this nation hazard its ease, its interest, and its power for the sake of a people so far away?

We fight because we must fight if we are to live in a world where every country can shape its own destiny. And only in such a world will our own freedom be finally secure.

This kind of a world will never be built by bombs and bullets. Yet the infirmities of man are such that force must often precede reason—and the waste of war, the works of peace.

We wish this were not so. But we must deal with the world as it is, if it is ever to be as we wish. . . . Let no one think retreat

. . . **April 7, 1965.** President Johnson explains rationale for widened war in speech at Johns Hopkins University . . . .

from Vietnam would bring an end to conflict. The battle would be renewed in one country and then another. The central lesson of our time is that the appetite of aggression is never satisfied. To withdraw from one battlefield means only to prepare for the next. We must say in South-East Asia—as we did in Europe—in the words of the Bible: "Hitherto shalt thou come, but no further."

—From an address by President Lyndon Johnson at Johns Hopkins University, April 7, 1965.

WASHINGTON, April 17—More than 15,000 students and a number of their elders picketed the White House in spring sunshine today, calling for an end of the fighting in Vietnam. Walking three and four abreast in orderly rows and carrying printed white signs, the students clogged the sidewalk. The principal occupant of the White House was at his ranch in Texas. In early afternoon, the marchers paraded to the Sylvan Theater, on the grounds of the Washington Monument, for a series of speeches. Then they walked down the Mall to the Capitol, bearing a petition for Congress. The demonstration was initated by Students for a Democratic Society, a left-leaning but non-Communist group with chapters on 63 campuses throughout the country. It had the support of several civil rights organizations, Women Strike for Peace and other groups. The supporting civil rights organizations included the Student Nonviolent Coordinating Committee . . .

Carol Holland, a 20-year-old student at Colby Junior Col-

. . . April 17, 1965. First major demonstration against the Vietnam War sponsored by Students for a Democratic Society (SDS) in Washington, D.C. . . . .

lege, said she had travelled all night by automobile with three other students and a professor.

"People always ask what a person can do," she said. "I'm just one person and I'm here to say I don't agree with what we're doing in Vietnam.". . .

Paul Booth, a 21-year-old spokesman for Students for a Democratic Society, outlined the aims of the demonstration. "We're really not just a peace group," he said. "We are working on domestic problems—civil rights, poverty, university reform. We feel passionately and angrily about things in America, and we feel that a war in Asia will destroy what we're trying to do here."

> —"15,000 White House Pickets Denounce Vietnam War," New York Times, April 18, 1965.

[T]hose who weep crocodile tears about "American boys" dying in the jungle overlook the fact that the American soldiers in Vietnam are not boys but men. Almost without exception the few thousand Americans who have the really dangerous jobs out in the boondocks are professional soldiers. A man does not become a professional soldier, after all, in order to avoid all risk.

After chatting with some of the American soldiers in the field in Vietnam, I scribbled in my notebook: "These guys seem so damn happy." This may sound fatuous, but it is true. Living on rice and noodles and chasing hard-core Communists may not be the average American's idea of happiness. But these men are not average Americans—they are regular soldiers by choice. They are "so damn happy" in part, I suspect, because they have at last escaped the elephantine Army bureaucracy and are on their own. But they are also happy because they are doing a job that needs doing, and they are doing it well, which is a pretty good recipe for happiness.

It is just plain silly, in short, to maintain that the American commitment in Vietnam places an intolerable strain on the United States, or even on the few thousand soldiers who are in the dangerous jobs there. These soldiers would be infuriated, to a man, by any official decision to withdraw the American commitment, and let South Vietnam go down the drain.

—*Stewart Alsop, "The Meaning of the Dead,"* Saturday Evening Post, *April 24, 1965.*

If one probes beneath the rationalizations for our military presence in South Vietnam, one finds as the dominant motivation the fear that if South Vietnam should go Communist, no nation threatened by Communism would entrust its protection to us. Thus one nation after the other would go Communist. In other words the Communization of South Vietnam would be the beginning of the end of the free world. We have even dignified this historic determinism with the name of a theory, the so-called "Domino Theory." It assumes that as South Vietnam goes so will Thailand, and as Thailand goes so will India, and so forth, until the whole world will have gone Communist. This theory is a slogan born of fear and of a misconception of history and politics. It is unsupported by any historic evidence. The Soviet Union went Communist in 1917 and China in 1949, but no other nation followed suit. In 1945, Poland and Hungary went Communist, but Finland did not, and all the Balkan States went Communist, but Greece did not. In 1948 Czechoslovakia went Communist, but no other nation did. In 1954 North Vietnam went Communist all by herself, and in 1960 or so Cuba went Communist without being followed by any other Latin American nation. Social and, more particularly, revolutionary change is not the mechanical result of imitation and prestige but of objective conditions peculiar to individual nations. It is, however, illuminating to note that the "Domino Theory" is but a replica of a vulgar Marxism which also believes in the inevitable spread of Communism from one country to the rest of the world.

—*Hans Morgenthau, "Russia, the U.S. and Vietnam," The New Republic, May 1, 1965.*

The "kill ratio" in Vietnam has increased from 2 to 1 in the government's favor to 6 to 1. And morale has perceptibly improved among the peasants in the coastal provinces, thanks to the new sense of security brought by the beefed-up Marine brigade at Da Nang air base.

Returning from an inspection tour of the Da Nang base, Gen. Wallace M. Greene, 58-year-old commandant of the Marine Corps, seemed undisturbed by reports that the Viet Cong are poised for a major offensive against the base. "Just let 'em try it," said Greene. "The Marine mission is to kill Viet Cong. They can't do it by sitting on their ditty boxes. I told them to find the Viet Cong and kill 'em. That's the way to carry out their mission."

And indeed, while the general was in South Vietnam earlier last week, the Marines obeyed their fighting orders by launching the first all-American heliborne raid of the war. Ten lum-

... **May 3–12, 1965.** 173rd Airborne Brigade arrives in South Vietnam, first U.S. Army combat unit committed to the war. . . **May 4, 1965.** President Johnson asks Congress to approve an additional $700 million appropriation for military involvement in Vietnam. . . . .

bering, dark-green helicopters swooped in on a suspected Viet Cong position; but it proved to be a false alarm. Meanwhile, a reconnaissance company tricked one guerrilla out into the open and when he tried to flee, the Marines chalked up another kill in South Vietnam.

—" 'The Mission Is to Kill,' " Newsweek, May 10, 1965.

SAIGON, South Vietnam, June 20—The Vietcong have lost considerable support among villagers in the areas under their control during the last six months, according to findings of independent American researchers.

The Communist guerrillas were said to have engendered dissatisfaction by the conscription of men for their military units, a heavy increase in taxation and punitive measures imposed on the population . . .

The findings of the survey are based on interviews by professional interrogators of Vietcong prisoners and defectors. The detailed interviews were carried out in such places as Government camps for defectors, and in jails and cages where Vietcong captives are held . . .

The latest survey is based on more than 150 interviews conducted this year. The results embrace the effects of United States' bombing of North Vietnam and employment of American jet fighters since February in operations in South Vietnam.

The current survey does not take account of the effects on the Vietcong of their apparent victories over Government troops during the last three weeks. The Vietcong have destroyed at

... **June 16, 1965.** Secretary of Defense Robert McNamara announces that 21,000 more U.S. troops are to be sent to Vietnam . . . .

least five Government battalions, which would presumably raise their morale.

—*"Vietcong Found Alienating Villagers,"* New York Times, June 21, 1965.

[T]he question inevitably arises: in the punishing tropic heat of Vietnam, is the regular American soldier—who traditionally carries a heavy pack, relies on trucks, aircraft or helicopters for mobility and expects three square meals a day—the proper opponent for the Viet Cong guerrilla who travels lightly on foot and can subsist for days on small quantities of rice?

To this U.S. military men reply that today's American soldier and marine is as well prepared as any fighting man in the world for waging guerrilla warfare. Brig. Gen. Ellis Williamson, 47, whose 173rd U.S. Airborne Brigade at Bien Hoa has been conducting increasingly aggressive operations in battalion strength, flatly declares: "We can go in and tear pure hell out of the Viet Cong."

—Newsweek, *July 5, 1965.*

The situation in South Vietnam is worse than a year ago (when it was worse than a year before that) . . . The VC main and local forces, reinforced by militia and guerrillas, have the initiative and, with large attacks (some in regimental strength), are hurting ARVN forces badly. . . . We must choose among three courses of action with respect to Vietnam all of which involve different probabilities, outcomes and costs:

. . . **June 28–30, 1965.** 173rd Airborne Brigade carries out first large-scale U.S. ground offensive northeast of Saigon; one U.S. soldier is killed, but no significant contact is made with the Vietcong. . . **July 8, 1965.** Henry Cabot Lodge resumes the post of U.S. Ambassador to South Vietnam. . . . .

a. Cut our losses and withdraw under the best conditions that can be arranged—almost certainly conditions humiliating the United States and very damaging to our future effectiveness on the world scene.

b. Continue at about the present level, with the U.S. forces limited to say 75,000, holding on and playing for breaks—a course of action which, because our position would grow weaker, almost certainly would confront us later with a choice between withdrawal and an emergency expansion of forces, perhaps too late to do any good.

c. Expand promptly and substantially the U.S. military pressure against the Viet Cong in the South and maintain the military pressure against the North Vietnamese in the North . . . This alternative would stave off defeat in the short run and offer a good chance of producing a favorable settlement in the longer run; at the same time it would imply a commitment to see a fighting war clear through at considerable costs in casualties and matériel and would make any later decision to withdraw even more difficult and even more costly than would be the case today. . . .

—Memorandum for President Lyndon Johnson from Secretary of Defense Robert McNamara, July 20, 1965.

There are wild animals in Vietnam—elephants, tigers and leopards as well as smaller game, including wildcats. Monkeys are found in the coastal forests. Crocodiles thrive in the delta region. There is much talk of snakes—cobras and such—but they are rarely seen.

Despite this rather forbidding prospect for the troops that are due here, the experience of those already serving in Vietnam is somewhat encouraging. For they have shown that an American

can perform well in jungle heat and rain, and can adapt himself quickly to the terrain, as anywhere else. . . .

[T]he question arises whether the Vietcong is not tired as well, since he has been fighting for a long time, too. And attached to that question is another: whether this wily master of ambush is really a master of jungle warfare.

The answer to the latter is a resounding "no" from the American forces here. "Vietcong successes are, for the most part, a reflection of the nature of the war rather than a reflection of any innate superiority as a jungle fighter," Maj. Thomas M. Henry, operations officer for the 5th Special Forces, pointed out. "The guerrilla has time to conserve his energy. He sets the stage for the battle."

The Vietcong, of course, have well-trained forces increasingly well equipped . . . The Vietcong can wait weeks—perhaps months—for a single ambush if they think it profitable and thus do not tax the energies of the men. Meanwhile, the South Vietnamese and Americans are expending energy searching for them. On the other hand, the Vietcong also have their weaknesses.

"Don't overrate the enemy," urged Capt. George Squilace, a 36-year-old Marine from New York City. "The Asian, and that includes the Vietcong in particular, is bothered by the heat and the jungle as much as we are—maybe worse.

"He is racked by the same ills and he does not often have adequate medicines. We have been fighting them and capturing them. They make plenty of mistakes."

—Jack Raymond, "When G.I. Joe Meets Ol' Charlie," New York Times Magazine, July 25, 1965.

. . . **August 3, 1965.** The U.S. Defense Department announces that the draft quota will be more than doubled in the next two months . . . .

"I got me a VC, man. I got at least two of them bastards."

The exultant cry followed a 10-second burst of automatic weapons fire yesterday, and the dull crump of a grenade exploding underground.

The Marines ordered a Vietnamese corporal to go down into the grenade-blasted hole to pull out their victims.

The victims were three children between 11 and 14—two boys and a girl. Their bodies were riddled with bullets . . .

"Oh my God," a young Marine exclaimed. "They're all kids."

—New York Herald-Tribune, *August 3, 1965.*

It was a week of arrivals and departures, of decision and determination. Into Cam Ranh Bay on South Viet Nam's bulging east coast slipped a grey-hulled U.S. troop transport, its decks aswarm with the "Screaming Eagles" of the U.S. 101st Airborne Division. Sentries on the dock paced impassively, their faces shadowed under their helmet liners, their M-14 rifles riding taut from the slings. As the transport neared the dock,
a cry went up from the 3,799 paratroopers: "Take a break! We're here!" The sentries, like veterans anywhere, smiled knowingly.

The sheer ebullience of that cry, tinged as it was with eagerness and naivete, was both sad and stirring. As the 101st's former commander—Ambassador Maxwell Taylor—was quick to point out, it will take far more than fighting spirit for the U.S. to succeed in Viet Nam. Hovering over the bay in a helicopter prior to his final departure for Washington, Taylor watched his old outfit land, then issued a soldierly warning. The Communist Viet Cong, he said, is "an enemy who is shrewd, well-trained, and with the guile of the American Indian during his best days."

— *"South Viet Nam, Status and Strategy,"* Time *magazine, August 6, 1965.*

Far out at sea, mariners puzzled over a molten glow in the eastern sky. Over the roar of the freeway, motorists heard the unmistakable crack of rifle fire, the chilling stutter of machine guns. Above city hall, billowing smoke from 1,000 fires hung like a cerement. From the air, whole sections of the sprawling city looked as if they had been blitzed.

The atmosphere reminded soldiers of embattled Saigon. Yet this, last week, was Los Angeles—the City of Angels, the "safe city," as its boosters like to call it, the city that has always taken pride in its history of harmonious racial relations.

Savagery replaced harmony with nightmarish suddenness. One evening white Angelenos had nothing to worry about but the humidity. The next—and for four nights after that— marauding mobs in the Negro suburb of Watts pillaged, burned and killed, while 500 policemen and 5,000 National Guardsmen struggled vainly to contain their fury. Hour after hour, the toll mounted: 27 dead at week's end, nearly 600 injured, 1,700 arrested, property damage well over $100 million . . . The riot was the worst in the city's history, one of the worst ever in the U.S. To help quell it, California's Governor Pat Brown broke off a vacation in Greece and hurried home. "From here it is awfully hard to direct a war," said Brown. "That's what this is."

— *"Races: Trigger of Hate,"* Time *magazine, August 20, 1965.*

. . . **August 31, 1965.** President Johnson signs into law a bill making it a federal crime to destroy or deface a draft card. . . . .

Four miles up the B-52s streaked through a Pacific sunrise. They were part of a 12-plane strike en route to bomb a target in South Vietnam's Iron Triangle, a Vietcong base 40 miles from Saigon.

The huge bombers took off from Guam, 2,800 miles away. Since June SAC [Strategic Air Command] has flown more than 55 missions from there against Vietcong targets. The Air Force has been accused of using a sledgehammer to do the job of a flyswatter. It points out, however, that employing the huge planes in tactical missions has great value. The B-52s can carpet a large area at one time, use radar to bomb with pinpoint accuracy by day or night. They can also operate in all kinds of weather from altitudes that render them safe from V.C. ground fire, and their heavy bombs can penetrate the deepest tunnels in which the V.C. take refuge.

—*"A Prayer, a Take-Off and the B-52 Strike Is On,"* Life *magazine, November 12, 1965.*

SAIGON, South Vietnam, November 18—A United States Army battalion was ambushed and mauled yesterday by several hundred North Vietnamese regulars in the Iadrang River valley, about 200 miles north of Saigon.

The ambush, involving 750 troops of the United States' First Cavalry Division (Airmobile), was the worst suffered so far by an American combat unit in Vietnam. A company at the center of the battalion was practically wiped out.

... **November 2, 1965.** Norman Morrison burns himself to death in front of the Pentagon to protest the war. . . **November 14–16, 1965.** Battle of the Ia Drang Valley, resulting in heavy North Vietnamese and U.S. casualties. . . . .

For five days the narrow valley, about seven miles from the Cambodia border, has been a scene of ferocious fighting between Airmobile units and the North Vietnamese 66th Regiment, estimated at 2,000 elite troops. . . .

Large numbers of American dead and wounded lay scattered this morning among trees, brush and patches of elephant grass alongside dead and wounded North Vietnamese who had fallen in hand-to-hand fighting. . . .

A United States military spokesman in Saigon described the American casualties as "moderate," but witnesses termed them very serious.

> —Neil Sheehan, "Battalion of G.I.'s Battered in Trap; Casualties High,"
> New York Times, November 19, 1965.

A Viet Cong attack on Americans is typically a brief hit-and-run affair: the enemy usually runs as soon as the surprise wears off and U.S. units start hitting back with concerted firepower. The siege at Plei Me last month seemed a notable exception to the rule, as Communist troops in force stood their ground in a prolonged fire fight. But again last week, in two fierce engagements near the "Iron Triangle" north of Saigon, Viet Cong troops surprised U.S. Army units—and then stayed around to boldly slug it out.

For the U.S., one of the bloodiest battles of the war began as a platoon of paratroopers of the 173rd Airborne cautiously threaded their way through an apparently deserted V.C. camp only 30 miles northeast of Saigon. It contained freshly dug fortifications, bamboo picnic tables, even a bathing hole. The trooper on "point," leading the way, spotted a pair of black pajamas drying on a tree, went over to pull them down. Precisely at the moment he touched them, four concealed Communist machine guns opened fire.

The first burst, close to the ground, caught the point man in both legs; then, veering upward, it ripped into the man behind—opening his stomach and chest and tearing off the top of his head. Another trooper, hit twice, managed to claw his way almost to the cover of a tree. But bullets chopped him down just as he reached for his .45. Only four of the 3rd Squad's twelve men survived unscathed.

> —*"South Viet Nam, a Time of Blood,"* Time *magazine, November 19, 1965.*

The man who commands all the Marines in Vietnam . . . is Major General Lewis Walt. Walt is a big man who calls to mind a rugged, much battered ice hockey player and who manages to look both weary and dangerous at the same time. The problems of fighting in Vietnam weigh on him pretty steadily. "No 'front,' no 'rear' and it is absolutely impossible to tell friend from enemy without a program—even *with* one," he said to us . . .

"I wonder who they're shooting at," says a Marine.

"Haven't you heard?" rejoins another. "There are bad guys out there—the ones in black hats, or at least they wear black pajamas."

"That's what really bothers me about this war," says a voice in the darkness. "Sometimes I feel like one of the bad guys. I mean, in World War II it was more clearcut. You know, the Nazis on one side and us on the other. But when we go into these *villes* and the people look at you in that sad kind of way they have, it's pretty hard for me to imagine I'm wearing a white hat and riding a white horse."

—Michael Mok, "In They Go to the Reality of This War," Life magazine, November 26, 1965.

The dramatic recent changes in the situation are on the military side. They are the increased infiltration from the North and the increased willingness of the Communist forces to stand and fight, even in large-scale engagements. The Ia Drang River Campaign in early November is an example. The Communists appear to have decided to increase their forces in SVN both by heavy recruitment in the South (especially in the Delta) and by infiltration of regular NVN forces from the North. . . . We have but two options, it seems to me. One is to go now for a compromise solution . . . and hold further deployments to a minimum. The other is to stick with our stated objectives and with the war, and provide what it takes in men and matériel. If it is decided not to move now toward a compromise, I recommend that the U.S. both send a substantial number of additional troops and very gradually intensify the bombing of NVN.

—Report by Secretary of Defense Robert McNamara on visit to Vietnam, November 30, 1965.

December 7, 1965—Our day starts at 4 A.M. We dress quickly and get outside for reveille in our shirtsleeves. Our teeth chatter from the cold, and I can't wait until they raise the flag and fire the gun salute. Why we don't put on hats and coats is a puzzle. Still trying to toughen us up, I suppose. We'll either turn to leather or die of pneumonia. We eat in our own barracks, which

. . . **November 27, 1965.** 35,000 march in Washington to protest the war . . . .

are one hell of a lot better than those at Dix. Everything is clean and orderly here. The dining hall reminds me of the cafeteria back at school. The food isn't bad either, but they give us less than five minutes to eat it.

The rest of the morning it's weapons classes, M-14 rifles. I was actually afraid to pick mine up at first. I've never handled a real gun before. And I don't like the idea now, knowing what it's supposed to do to a person. I don't know. I just can't imagine myself killing anyone with it. I keep dropping the damned thing, and [Sgt.] Crouch eats me out each time. He was really pissed off today. "You clumsy idiot," he hollered at me. "You're here to learn to kill! And this is what you will kill with! You better learn that fast or the VC will blow your ass to hell! Drop it in combat and you're dead! You get that?"

"Got it, *sir*."

—David Parks, GI Diary *(1968)*.

DECEMBER 31, 1965:

U.S. Troop Level in South Vietnam—184,300
Total U.S. Killed in Vietnam War—2,265

Washington is not trying to push Ho Chi Minh into an agreement formally admitting defeat. After all, he has not yet been defeated. But for negotiations to yield any real results, the Communists would have to admit tacitly that they cannot force

. . . **December 16, 1965.** General Westmoreland requests reinforcements to bring U.S. troop levels to over 400,000 by the end of 1966. . . **December 25, 1965.** President Johnson suspends Operation Rolling Thunder as part of a "peace offensive" seeking a negotiated settlement to the war . . . .

the U.S. out, and thus conclude that they might as well cut their losses under some face-saving formula. Should the Communists ever reach that point, it is entirely possible that it would not lead them to the conference table at all, but that the war would end in a military stalemate and the gradual petering out of guerrilla attacks—as they petered out without ceremony in Greece, the Philippines, Malaya and the Congo.

> —"Is There Really Anything to Negotiate?", Time magazine, January 14, 1966.

Swept by the sand, tense in the face of the precarious and unexpected aspects of this treacherous war, these soldiers wait as their commander calls for air support to enable his squads to move forward. They are a unit of the 1st Cavalry Division (Airmobile) operating in the central highlands of Vietnam.

The lull that had marked the war since President Johnson launched his peace offensive six weeks ago was over. The 1st Cav has pushed off on Operation Masher—one prong of the biggest offensive ever mounted in the central highlands, control of which has become the tactical key to the war. The second phase of the offensive, called Operation Double Eagle, involved 4,000 U.S. Marines in the largest amphibious landing since Inchon in the Korean War. Altogether 20,000 American, South Vietnamese and South Korean troops were participating in the offensive aimed at trapping an estimated 8,000 North

... **January 24, 1966.** U.S. 1st Air Cavalry Division and allied units launch Operation Masher/White Wing/Thang Phong II in Binh Dinh Province, a month-and-a-half-long search-and-destroy operation, the most ambitious to date. . . **January 31, 1966.** U.S. bombing of North Vietnam resumes. . . **February 4, 1966.** Senate Foreign Relations Committee begins hearings on war in Vietnam. . . **February 6–9, 1966.** President Johnson flies to Honolulu, where he meets with South Vietnamese leaders Thieu, Ky, etc.........................

Vietnamese regulars and Vietcong soldiers in the coastal area
about 300 miles north of Saigon. . . .

> —"On with the War and 'Operation Masher,' " Life magazine, February
> 11, 1966.

Never before had the Communists been hit so hard and in so
many places at one time. From south of Saigon to coastal
Quang Ngai, over 25,000 allied troops stalked the Reds in six
separate operations. It was far and away the biggest battle week
of the war . . .

Far and away the most important operation was White Wing,
led by 1st Air Cav Colonel Hal G. Moore, 43, a lean, laconic
Kentuckian who earned a battlefield promotion at bloody Ia
Drang last November. In that fight, he held together a single
infantry battalion surrounded by three battalions of North Vietnamese regulars. This time he was the aggressor, leading the
largest allied force of the war. . . .

For four years the pleasant coastal plain of Binh Dinh has
been a private Communist demiparadise of palm-topped villages and emerald paddies. But underneath paradise were the
ubiquitous mole holes of the Viet Cong—an estimated 3,000
strong in the area. . . .

The enemy was waiting. Almost at once five choppers were
shot down. "We're in a hornet's nest!" radioed Captain John
Fesmire. Soon, both his mortar platoon leader and radio operator were killed, his company was scattered to the north of the
helidrop zone, and a rescue company sent to his assistance was
pinned down by cross-fire as well. One of Fesmire's lieuten-
ants, his right leg smashed by machine gun bullets, propped
himself against a sand dune and, with his back to the battle,
called in artillery fire by the sound of the exploding shells. The

sergeant who had taken over the weapons platoon was trapped near a machine gun nest. He had his mortar tube—but no base plate, no plotting board, no aiming stakes, nor forward observer. With only six rounds of ammunition, he watched five explode harmlessly some distance from the target. Then he lifted his last round, kissed it, and fired. It leveled the machine gunners' hut. . . .

Unable to escape, the Communists, now identified as two regiments—one regular North Vietnamese, one partly Viet Cong—had to fight, to their sorrow. By the third day of White Wing, nearly 400 of the enemy had been killed, against relatively light casualties by the allies.

—*"The Biggest Week,"* Time *magazine, February 11, 1966.*

"Now those Vietnamese are more than names. Now when President Johnson reads the raw cables from Saigon, those Vietnamese leaders will be more than just names. He'll hear their voices, see their faces. Every decision he makes will have that visibility quotient in it." Thus a close presidential aide described what is probably the largest benefit to come out of last week's summit meeting between U.S. and South Vietnamese officials.

Johnson was highly impressed with the Vietnamese delegation, especially Chief of State Nguyen Van Thieu and Prime Minister Nguyen Cao Ky—and they were impressed with him. "What pleased him most was that these military men had a social conscience," one of Johnson's staff said.

—*"Now Those Vietnamese Are More Than Names,"* Life *magazine, February 18, 1966.*

By summer the effects of all our efforts should really begin to be felt on the battlefields. A point comes in a war when momentum develops; cumulative and multiplying effects spread across a whole theater; one action goes well, and things seem to go better in half a dozen other places. The momentum was running strongly for the Vietcong in early 1965. It could be running strongly for our side in late 1966.

Barring a negotiated settlement, nobody will ever be able to name the exact date when the present phase of the war came to an end. But the day should come, late this year or next, when it will be possible to add up some such set of facts as this: dwindling southbound traffic on the Ho Chi Minh Trail for several months; increase in northbound traffic; no firm contact with a full V.C. regiment or battalion for several weeks; occasional capture of V.C. or North Vietnam "regulars" now operating with small local guerrilla units; extension of government control to territory containing 75% of the population; decline of V.C. "incidents" within this territory. . . .

—Hedley Donovan, "Vietnam: The War Is Worth Winning," Life magazine, February 25, 1966.

WASHINGTON, Feb. 28—The commander of United States Marine forces in South Vietnam said today that he had told President Johnson that he needed more forces in his area.

Maj. Gen Lewis W. Walt, whose Third Marine Division operates in the northern part of South Vietnam, said that these additional forces were necessary to secure areas pacified by United States military action. There are 40,000 Marines in Vietnam. Overall United States strength is about 205,000.

Speaking at a news conference, General Walt indicated that a recent intensive three-week action by 6,000 Marines aimed at clearing a 500-square-mile area south of the Danang Air Force Base was not a complete success because of his inability to leave Marines behind to protect the area.

The operation, called Double Eagle, was described by the Defense Department as the biggest amphibious operation since the Korean war. . . . Among the accomplishments of the action, General Walt cited the killing of 309 guerrillas, the administration of medical aid to 1,000 civilians, the distribution of food, and in general, the improvement of Marine relations with the people in the area.

Where the Vietcong had given the civilian population "a rough time," General Walt said, "we did nothing but good."

He said he would have liked "to stay longer" and to have left some men behind, "but I couldn't because we don't have enough Marines at the present time."

—Richard Eder, "U.S. Marine Chief in Vietnam Wants Additional Forces," New York Times, March 1, 1965.

WASHINGTON, March 1—Both houses of Congress over-whelmingly approved today the $4.8 billion military authorization bill to provide additional funds for the Vietnam war.

The Senate acted after voting, 92 to 5, to table, and thus kill, an amendment offered by Senator Wayne Morse that would have repealed the 1964 Gulf of Tonkin resolution.

—E.W. Kenworthy, "Congress Passes $4.8 Billion Fund for Vietnam War," New York Times, March 2, 1966.

The folk-rock of anti-Vietnam war ballads has been drowned out by a best-selling patriotic blood-churner. Called *The Ballad of the Green Berets*, it is a march-beat salute to Americans who

die in Vietnam "for the oppressed," and it was written by Barry
Sadler, 25, who served as a combat medic with the U.S. Army
Special Forces in Vietnam. The Special Forces, trained for
unconventional jungle warfare, were special favorites of President Kennedy, who overruled Pentagon objections to let them
wear rakish green berets.

Sadler wrote his songs in Vietnam. When he was wounded
and sent back to Fort Bragg, N.C., he recorded the songs for
RCA Victor. So far his album and single record of *The Ballad*
have sold two million copies, and Sadler's first venture into the
alien jungle of Tin Pan Alley could earn him $250,000.

—"Hail to 'Green Berets,' " Life *magazine, March 4, 1966.

Cash Box Top Ten Singles, 1966

1. The Ballad of the Green Berets—S/Sgt. Barry Sadler
2. California Dreamin'—The Mamas & the Papas
3. The Sounds of Silence—Simon & Garfunkel
4. Sunny—Bobby Hebb
5. Strangers in the Night—Frank Sinatra
6. You Can't Hurry Love—The Supremes
7. A Groovy Kind of Love—The Mindbenders
8. I Got You—James Brown
9. Little Red Riding Hood—Sam the Sham & the Pharoahs
10. Good Lovin'—The Young Rascals

HUE, South Vietnam, Wednesday, June 1—A screaming mob
of about 1,000 students sacked and burned the United States
Consulate building today. Yelling and blowing whistles, the

... **April 12, 1966.** Strategic Air Command (SAC) B-52s based in Guam are used for the first
time in raids on North Vietnam . . . .

students ripped down portraits of President Johnson and carried off two American flags while the building burned and other students threw rocks at the windows.

A company of South Vietnam Army troops, in full battle gear, fled when the students approached.

—*"Student Mob in Hue Burns American Consular Office,"* New York Times, *June 1, 1966.*

OMAHA, June 30—President Johnson said today that United States air strikes on military targets in North Vietnam "will continue to impose a growing burden and a high price on those who wage war against the freedom of their neighbors."

The resolute tone of Mr. Johnson's remarks, made in a speech, indicated no wavering in his decision to step up the tempo of the war to convince North Vietnam that it cannot win and should seek to negotiate a settlement.

It was the President's first pronouncement alluding to the important escalation of the war signaled by the United States bombing raids yesterday on fuel dumps close to Hanoi and Haiphong. . . .

The President said that he had seen a young man today carrying a sign saying, "Get out of Vietnam."

"I thought," Mr. Johnson said of him, "the thing you want most—to get out of Vietnam—is being postponed a little longer because of you and your sign. I'm not angry. I'm not

. . . **June 18, 1966.** General Westmoreland requests reinforcements to bring U.S. troop levels to over 500,000 by the end of 1967. . . **June 29, 1966.** President Johnson authorizes bombing of Hanoi and Haiphong oil installations . . . .

even sorrowful. But I sometimes think, God forgive them for they know not what they do."

—*John D. Pomfret, "President Vows to Press Punishing of Aggressors; Hanoi Area Bombed Again,"* New York Times, July 1, 1966.

Three Army privates who have orders to report this month for embarkation to Vietnam said yesterday they would not go.

They denounced the war as "immoral, illegal and unjust," and likened the United States' involvement in some ways to the Nazi aggression in Europe.

The three are on furlough now and will report to Oakland, Calif., as they have been ordered, but they said that they would refuse to board a troop transport for Vietnam. . . .

Pvt. Dennis Mora, 25 years old of New York City, a former social worker for the Welfare Department, read from a joint statement in which the three soldiers declared: "We have made our decision. We will not be part of this unjust, immoral and illegal war.

"We want no part of a war of extermination. We oppose the criminal waste of American lives and resources. We refuse to go to Vietnam." . . . The two other soldiers were Pfc. James A. Johnson, 20, of New York, and Pvt. David A. Samas, 20, of Modesto, Calif. . . .

The three soldiers identified themselves as members of the 142nd Signal Battalion, who were given furloughs on June 10, which are to last through July 13. At that time they are to report at the Oakland, California Army Terminal for travel to Vietnam. . . .

The three made it clear they were not pacifists. They agreed, they said, that they would have fought against the Nazis, but they appeared undecided whether they would have fought in the Korean war . . .

The soldiers chose for their lawyer Stanley Faulkner of 9 East 40th Street, near Fifth Avenue, who represented Robert Luftig, an Army cook who contended the war in Vietnam was illegal and refused to go. His case is before the United States Court of Appeals. . . .

Mr. Faulkner said that he was contending in part that the war in Vietnam had never been declared by Congress, that it violated the United Nations charter, which was binding on the United States, and that the three men were being forced by the Government to commit illegal acts if they should go to Vietnam.

—Martin Arnold, "3 Soldiers Hold News Conference to Announce They Won't Go to Vietnam," New York Times, July 1, 1966.

SAIGON, South Vietnam, Monday, August 8—Seven United States warplanes were lost over North Vietnam yesterday, a record for American aircraft losses in a single day in the war.

The losses brought to a total of 326 the number of American planes that have crashed or been shot down over North Vietnam since that country was first bombed in August of 1964.

Five Air Force F-105 Thunderchief jet fighter bombers and one Navy propeller-driven A-1E Skyraider were shot down by enemy ground fire . . . This morning a military spokesman disclosed that another aircraft, an Air Force RF-101 Voodoo

July 15, 1966. U.S. Marines and ARVN soldiers launch Operation Hastings against North Vietnamese troops threatening Quangtri Province. . . **August 3, 1966.** U.S. Marines launch Operation Prairie against North Vietnamese forces near Demilitarized Zone (DMZ) . . . .

photo reconnaissance plane, disappeared yesterday on a mission northwest of Hanoi . . . The five Thunderchiefs lost yesterday crashed in the vicinity of Hanoi and Haiphong. The Skyraider went down south of Thanhhoa in the panhandle region of southern North Vietnam.

The pilot and electronics officer of one F-105 bailed out and were later rescued from the South China Sea, but the six other airmen involved were listed as missing in action.

> —"7 U.S. Planes Lost in North Vietnam, Most in Any Day," New York
> Times, August 8, 1966.

SAIGON, South Vietnam, Aug. 7—A study prepared by the United States Marine Corps holds that North Vietnam can continue indefinitely to absorb casualties in South Vietnam at the present rate.

About 40,000 North Vietnamese troops are believed by allied intelligence to be in the South, and the study suggests that Hanoi has enough manpower to maintain this level by infiltration despite allied operations. . . .

If they are correct, the war in Vietnam could last well into the next decade. Many analysts question whether either the South Vietnamese public or the American public is prepared to support so long a struggle.

> —R.W. Apple, Jr., "Hanoi Can Absorb Present Loss Rate, Marine Study
> Says," New York Times, August 8, 1966.

The problem of desertion from the ranks has long given the South Vietnamese army nearly as much trouble as the Commu-

. . . September 6–9, 1966. Fort Hood Three are court-martialed at Fort Dix for disobeying orders to go to Vietnam . . . .

nist enemy. Some 37,000 regular, regional and popular governmental forces deserted in 1963, twice that many the next year, and 113,000 last year. During the first six months of this year, 67,000 went over the hill, a shocking annual rate of more than one man in every five under arms.

— "Shaping Up," Time magazine, September 9, 1966.

The terrain was as tough as any the U.S. Marines had ever contested. It combined the horror of a Guadalcanal jungle with the exhausting steepness of the slopes at Chapultepec. Added to that were fusillades of bullets as ferocious as at Tarawa and showers of shrapnel that turned the forest into a tropical Belleau Wood. But "the Rockpile," as Vietnam's latest big battleground has come to be called, is weirdly unique. There, just south of the inaccurately named Demilitarized Zone, a task force of six Marine battalions has been battling two entire divisions of North Vietnamese regulars whose apparent aim is to invade Quang Tri province. So far the Reds have failed. . . .

Key to the fighting is "the Rock," a jagged, 750-ft. fang of granite that thrusts upward at the intersection of three river valleys and two enemy trails. During July's Operation Hasting, the Marines established a reconnaissance post atop the Rock, and a lone sniper fed by airdrops of C rations controlled the area. Now it is a Marine battalion command post, under almost steady siege. Across from the Rock rears the Razorback—a steep ridge whose sides are pocked with caves dug by the Japanese in World War II, but now occupied by North Vietnamese. Several hundred yards below the Rock the Reds have

. . . **September 11, 1966.** South Vietnam holds election for Constituent Assembly
. . . **September 19, 1966.** Pope Paul VI appeals for peace in Vietnam . . . .

dug "spider holes" from which they lob mortar fire and mount ambushes. Two miles to the south stands Hill 400, dominating the Rockpile and infested with Reds. Last week the Marines moved simultaneously against the Razorback and Hill 400. By week's end, both were in their hands.

—*"South Viet Nam: The Rockpile,"* Time *magazine, October 7, 1966.*

Vietnam . . . has become the hinge on which the American Asian presence turns. A U.S. failure there could have far-reaching results. At the very least, the nations of Asia would be inclined to detach themselves somewhat from the United States, fearful that it lacked the power and resolution to guarantee their security. Defeat in Vietnam moreover might well induce the U.S. itself to begin a slow withdrawal from Asia . . . Paradoxically enough, however, success in Vietnam would bring problems of its own. For the end of large-scale fighting in South Vietnam would be only the beginning of the real war there—and throughout much of underdeveloped Asia as well. That war—against poverty, ignorance and disease— may well last beyond the lifetime of most middle-aged Americans.

It seems highly probable, in fact, that over the next few decades at least, America's greatest concerns will be with Asia, rather than with the European nations.

—*"U.S. in Asia: Is This the Dawn of a New Pacific Era?",* Newsweek, *October 31, 1966.*

. . . **October 10–14, 1966.** Secretary of Defense Robert McNamara visits Vietnam on fact-finding mission. . . **October 15, 1966.** U.S. troops launch a search-and-destroy mission named Operation Attleboro in Tayninh Province near the Cambodian border, meeting strong resistance in battles in early November. . . **October 26, 1966.** President Johnson visits U.S. troops in Camranh Bay in South Vietnam . . . .

HANOI, North Vietnam, Dec. 24—Late in the afternoon of this drizzly Christmas Eve the bicycle throngs on the roads leading into Hanoi increased.

Riding sidesaddle behind husbands were hundreds of slender young Hanoi wives returning to the city from evacuation to spend Christmas with their families. Hundreds of mothers had small children perched on the backs of bicycles—children being returned to the city for reunions during the Christmas cease-fire.

In Hanoi's Catholic churches mass was celebrated, and here and there in the small foreign quarter there were more elaborate holiday observances. . . .

But this random evidence of Christmas spirit did not convey the mood of North Vietnam's capital, at least not as it seemed to an unexpected observer from the United States.

The mood of Hanoi seemed much more that of a wartime city going about its business briskly, energetically, purposefully. Streets are lined with cylindrical one-man air-raid shelters set in the ground at 10-foot intervals.

The shelters are formed of prestressed concrete with concrete lids left ajar for quick occupancy—and they are reported to have been occupied quite a bit in recent days with the sudden burst of United States air raids. . . .

Christmas Eve found residents in several parts of Hanoi still picking over the wreckage of homes said to have been damaged in the United States raids of Dec. 13 and 14. United States officials have contended that no attacks in built-up or residen-

. . . **November 7, 1966.** Secretary of Defense Robert McNamara is surrounded by student antiwar demonstrators when he attempts to leave Harvard University after a speaking engagement. . . **December 25, 1966.** *New York Times* correspondent Harrison Salisbury creates a stir with dispatch from Hanoi detailing damage to civilian neighborhoods from U.S. bombing; Pentagon calls reports of damage exaggerated . . . .

tial Hanoi have been authorized or carried out. They have also suggested that Hanoi residential damage could have been caused by defensive surface-to-air missiles that misfired or fell short. . . .

This correspondent is no ballistics specialist, but inspection of several damaged sites and talks with witnesses make it clear that Hanoi residents certainly believe they were bombed by United States planes, that they certainly observed United States planes overhead and that damage certainly occurred right in the center of town. . . . Contrary to the impression given by United States communiqués, on-the-spot inspection indicates that American bombing has been inflicting considerable civilian casualties in Hanoi and its environs for some time past.

> —Harrison E. Salisbury, "A Visitor to Hanoi Inspects Damage Laid to U.S. Raids," New York Times, December 25, 1966.

DECEMBER 31, 1966:

U.S. Troop Level in South Vietnam—385,300
Total U.S. Killed in Vietnam War—8,409

Two thousand Marines landed in the Delta last week and got the inevitable taste of what campaigning in the Delta is like. They waded into a mangrove swampland, up to their waists in

... **January 2, 1967.** USAF jets shoot down 7 Mig-21s over North Vietnam in largest air battle of the war to date... **January 8, 1967.** U.S. and ARVN troops launch search-and-destroy operation near Saigon named Operation Cedar Falls, which uncovers a massive tunnel complex in the Viet Cong stronghold known as the Iron Triangle ....

water and muck. From the standpoint of modern arms, the conditions the Delta imposes on fighting seem to be the work of a malevolent genius.

First, there is the sheer baffling problem of a place to stand. The Delta's pervasive muck, cross-hatched with narrow paddy dikes and laced with meandering canals and streamlets, grudges the space to pitch a shelter half, much less a division CP [Command Post] or an airfield. Indeed, there are few landing places in the Delta—all small, none capable of handling jets or heavy transports.

Handmaiden to the impasse of place is the question of what to use for tools. The wondrously versatile helicopter, which can sit down to rest nearly anywhere, is being used extensively already. But there is little or no footing in the Delta for tanks or heavy armor . . . The only U.S. vessels now plying the Delta waterways are the ingenious but fragile patrol boats built of fiber glass and powered with water-jet engines to keep draft to the minimum. Even these stick to the main channels. The creeks and canals entering either side are still the exclusive province of the native man-powered sampan. . . . There is another specific limitation to fighting in the Delta, for which there is no easy remedy: the swarm of population. "This war is right in the middle of more than five million people," says Brig. General William R. Desobry, senior American adviser to the Vietnamese troops in the Delta. "We are going to have to be very discriminating with our firepower."

—*"New U.S. Front in a Widening War: The Delta, Steamy, Teeming Heartland of the Vietcong," Life magazine, January 13, 1967.*

Nothing I had read, no photographs I had seen prepared me for the immensity of the American effort. It is impressive enough to read that we have committed more troops to Vietnam than were necessary to fight the North Koreans and Chinese combined in 1950 and to realize that each American soldier carries six times the firepower he had in World War II. But the fantastic expense of Vietnam—$20 billion last year, $10 billion beyond the estimate—can only be comprehended in the viewing.

Literally everything is Texas-sized, from the new "Pentagon West" ($25 million), which will provide offices for most of the 68 American generals stationed in Saigon, to a cantonment for 60,000 troops under construction at Long Binh ($90 million). Both projects should be ready for occupancy this fall.

In World War II the engineers of Seabees would level a 3,000-foot strip of topsoil, lay some pierced steel plank and report the airfield ready to receive planes. With jet planes it's different. Jets need dust-free, 10,000-foot-long strips of aluminum or concrete—which cost $5 million or more. We have built nine new jet landing fields between Da Nang and Saigon. The total number of airfields in South Vietnam is now 282, one of the highest in the world. . . .

In less than two years the number of American troops based on Vietnamese soil has leaped from 25,000 to more than 400,000. To support them 150 cargo vessels are always on the seas or at the docks. The trouble was the lack of docks, which often forced ships to wait a month to unload at Saigon. Okay, build deep-water piers. Saigon has three, and nearby New Port will have four. The big Marine Corps base at Da Nang had no piers; all supplies had to be unloaded by lighter. So we dredged channels and built three piers which, with attached facilities such as a four-lane concrete bridge, will cost $120 million. Development of the great natural harbor at Cam Ranh Bay, the site of President Johnson's visit last November, will come cheaper—only $110 million.

One evening I flew from the demilitarized zone down to Saigon, about three quarters of the length of this 900-mile string bean of a country. Much of the coast was lit up by flares; artillery shells twinkled in 40 or 50 different spots. No battles were being fought that night but the Vietcong, if present, presumably were being kept awake and the interdicting fire prevented them from traveling certain routes in case they intended going that way. This lavish use of firepower, whether effective or not, contributes to the cost of killing the enemy, which is calculated at $400,000 per soldier—including 75 bombs and 150 artillery shells for each corpse.

—*Robert Sherrod, "Notes on a Monstrous War,"* Life *magazine, January 27, 1967.*

The men had assembled by their planes in the darkness and as the tropic dawn came rushing up, the sky changing in minutes from deep red to flowing white, each had strapped himself into almost a hundred pounds of gear—main chutes and reserves, ammo and weapons, radios and grenades and Claymore mines and antitank rockets. They were men of the Second Battalion, 503rd Airborne Infantry Regiment, 173rd Airborne Brigade and they were about to make the first U.S. combat jump of the Vietnam War. . . .

The U.S. parachute jump kicked off "Operation Junction City," the largest major action of the war. The paratroopers were one element of a multi-divisional force totalling 30,000 men. Their mission was to throw a horseshoe-shaped net

. . . **February 8, 1967.** U.S. halts bombing of North Vietnam during Tet holiday . . . **February 13, 1967.** U.S. resumes bombing of North Vietnam. . . **February 16, 1967.** Communist ground fire shoots down 13 U.S. helicopters, a new record for one day . . . . . .

around the northwest part of War Zone C—the 1,000-square-mile Vietcong jungle stronghold near the Cambodian border, 75 miles northwest of Saigon. They were to find and destroy any Vietcong trapped inside, and search out what was believed to be the headquarters of the entire V.C. political and military high command. The 800 paratroopers belonged to a unit that in World War II had jumped to help retake Corregidor. Now it was making the first U.S. combat jump since Korea. . . .

The C-130s passed low over their landing zone—code-named AO-Red—at nine o'clock. The first men out of the first plane were brigade commander Brig. General John R. Deane and Lt. Colonel Sigholtz. As their chutes popped, all alone in the blue sky, Sigholtz could hear sniper bullets going *snap*, *snap*, *snap* at him from down below. An armed helicopter arced around and made a run down the DZ [Drop Zone], its machine guns ripping into the treeline, and after that the sniper didn't shoot anymore. . . . Chief Warrant Officer Melvin stood in the drop zone looking up at the sky. He had added AO-Red to the list of his own combat jumps—Gela, Salerno, Ste.-Mere-Eglise and Nijmegen. . . . Elated, Melvin looked for Sigholtz at the assembly point and found his colonel elated too. A few sprains, but not a serious injury to any of his men. The snipers had been beaten back, almost 800 men had hit the ground within 10 minutes and Sigholtz's planning had worked so well that 90% of his battalion was in position within an hour. "Colonel," Melvin reported, "we got everything here—intact."

"Mister Melvin," Sigholtz replied with a grin, "everything worked the way we *planned* it."

The same note of complete satisfaction can hardly be sounded yet for the operation as a whole. Troops did discover some base areas, stockpiled with everything from ammunition to 1,750 rubber erasers. But not until the end of its first week did

any American unit make substantial contact with the enemy—
a company of the 1st Infantry Division took heavy casualties in
a six-hour battle near the Cambodian border in which more
than 200 V.C. dead were counted. Beyond this action the GIs
had mostly pursued elusive shadows through the jungle, inflicting scattered casualties and taking a few themselves from
mines and booby traps.

—*Don Moser, "US Paratroopers in a Stepped-up War, Battle Jump,"* Life
magazine, March 10, 1967.

There is . . . a very obvious and almost facile connection between the war in Vietnam and the struggle I, and others, have
been waging in America. A few years ago there was a shining
moment in that struggle. It seemed as if there was a real
promise of hope for the poor—both black and white—through
the Poverty Program. Then came the build-up in Vietnam, and I
watched the program broken and eviscerated as if it were some
idle political plaything of a society gone mad on war, and I
knew that America would never invest the necessary funds or
energies in rehabilitation of its poor so long as Vietnam continued to draw men and skills and money like some demonic,
destructive suction tube. So I was increasingly compelled to see
the war as an enemy of the poor and to attack it as such.

Perhaps the more tragic recognition of reality took place
when it became clear to me that the war was doing far more
than devastating the hopes of the poor at home. It was sending
their sons and their brothers and their husbands to fight and to
die in extraordinarily high proportions relative to the rest of the

. . . **March 22, 1967.** Thailand agrees to allow U.S. B-52s to use its territory for launching
raids on North and South Vietnam. . . . .

population. We were taking the young black men who had been crippled by our society and sending them 8000 miles away to guarantee liberties in Southeast Asia which they had not found in Southwest Georgia and East Harlem. So we have been repeatedly faced with the cruel irony of watching Negro and white boys on TV screens as they kill and die together for a nation that has been unable to seat them together in the same schools. So we watch them in brutal solidarity burning the huts of a poor village, but we realize that they would never live on the same block in Detroit. I could not be silent in the face of such cruel manipulation of the poor . . .

As I have walked among the desperate and rejected and angry young men, I have told them Molotov cocktails and rifles would not solve their problems. I have tried to offer them my deepest compassion while maintaining my conviction that social change comes most meaningfully through non-violent action. But, they asked, what about Vietnam? They asked if our own nation wasn't using massive doses of violence to solve its problems, to bring about the changes it wanted. Their questions hit home, and I knew that I could never again raise my voice against the violence of the oppressed in the ghettos without having first spoken clearly to the greatest purveyor of violence in the world today—my own government.

> —Martin Luther King, Jr., "Declaration of Independence from the War in Vietnam," speech delivered April 4, 1967.

April 6, 1967—Greenfield got it today. It was our first day on Operation Hammer, a search-and-destroy deal. . . . It was quiet and we were rumbling along beside a wood line that separated us from a shallow river. Greenfield was sitting to my left just behind the driver. Suddenly two shots whined over our heads.

We scrambled over the top of the track and jumped down into the hatch, leaving just our heads exposed. I called the mortar platoon leader and reported that we were receiving sniper fire. But as usual there were choppers overhead and so the mortars were held. The artillery was pounding away from the rear, and we let go with our 50- and 60-cals. I heard Thomas order a cease-fire over the earphones, and the guns stopped. Then the snipers opened up again. There was a cracking sound to my left. I turned just in time to see blood gushing through a hole in Greenfield's helmet. He'd been hit and his head disappeared beneath the top of the track. I jumped down beside him, but Lt. Wyeth was already reaching for a bandage to try and stop the bleeding. When Greenfield started choking on his own blood, Wyeth stuck his fingers between his teeth so the blood could run out of his mouth. "Hold on, Greenfield. Hold on. You're gonna make it." His head was moving. Our guns were blasting the wood line again. I called Thomas for a chopper to take Greenfield out, and he said one was already on the way to pick up a Third Platoon leader who'd been hit.

A medic from another track jumped in to give first aid. He tried to open a morphine can with a key and it broke off. "Oh, shit!" He tried to pull the top of the can off with his bare hand and cut himself. "Shit! Shit! Shit!" Now *his* blood was all over the place.

Sachs, looking sick, said, "He's dead, man, he's dead!"

The choppers came in, firing at the wood line. Our guns were going full blast. We carried Greenfield to a chopper and the medic got in with him. I knew that was the last of Greenfield. No one could survive a wound like that. Another good Joe gone. . . . Poor Greenfield. Just a few more inches to the left and it would have been me. Maybe tomorrow will be my day. Who knows? Only yesterday he was talking about the girl back home he wanted to marry. He was a simple guy. He wanted to be a carpenter.

—*David Parks, GI Diary (1968).*

Thousands of antiwar demonstrators marched through the streets of Manhattan yesterday and then massed in front of the United Nations building to hear United States policy in Vietnam denounced.

The Police Department's Office of Community Relations said that police officers at the scene estimated the number of demonstrators outside the United Nations at "between 100,000 and 125,000."... It was the largest peace demonstration staged in New York since the Vietnam war began. It took four hours for all the marchers to leave Central Park for the United Nations Plaza.

The parade was led by the Rev. Dr. Martin Luther King, Jr., Dr. Benjamin Spock, the pediatrician, and Harry Belafonte, the singer, as well as several other civil rights and religious figures, all of whom linked arms as they moved out of the park at the head of the line.

The marchers—who had poured into New York on chartered buses, trains and cars from cities as far away as Pittsburgh, Cleveland and Chicago—included housewives from Westchester, students and poets from the Lower East Side, priests and nuns, doctors, businessmen and teachers.

As they began trooping out of Central Park toward Fifth

... **April 7, 1967.** Secretary of Defense Robert McNamara announces plans for constructing a fortified barrier south of the DMZ to cut off infiltration of supplies and men from North Vietnam... **April 15, 1967.** 300,000 antiwar protesters march in New York City, 50,000 in San Francisco, in largest protests to date. . . . .

Avenue, some of the younger demonstrators chanted: "Hell no, we won't go," and "Hey, Hey, L.B.J., How Many Kids Did You Kill Today."

Most of the demonstrators, however, marched silently as they passed equally silent crowds of onlookers. . . .

In his speech at the United Nations rally, Dr. King repeatedly called on the United States to "honor its word" and "stop the bombing of North Vietnam."

—*Douglas Robinson, "100,000 Rally at U.N. Against Vietnam War,"*
New York Times, April 16, 1967.

In the far northwestern corner of South Vietnam, two battalions of U.S. Marines fought in a point-blank 12-day battle—their toughest of the war. At stake was Khe Sanh Valley, a key channel through which the enemy hoped to launch a major offensive. An isolated U.S. and South Vietnamese force had held the valley but, dug into the hills above, two North Vietnamese regiments were hurrying to get long-range weapons in place. The Marines hit first—attacking three heavily fortified hills: 861, 881 South and North (each named for its height in meters above sea level) with air strikes, artillery and on foot. . . . The high-priority victory at Khe Sanh (the Marines suffered 900 casualties and by last week had resumed contact with the enemy a few miles north of the original battle site)

. . . **April 18, 1967.** General Westmoreland asks that U.S. troop levels in South Vietnam be increased to nearly 700,000 men. . . **April 24–May 5, 1967.** U.S. Marines suffer heavy casualties in battle for control of hilltops near Khesanh airstrip. . . **May 1, 1967.** Ellsworth Bunker is appointed U.S. Ambassador to South Vietnam. . . **May 8, 1967.** U.S. base at Conthien is attacked by North Vietnamese, with heavy casualties on both sides. . . **May 15, 1967.** North Vietnamese launch heavy attacks against U.S. Marine bases near DMZ; fighting continues through late May . . . .

reflected the sharpened tempo of the war . . . The North Vietnamese had massed several fresh divisions near the so-called
Demilitarized Zone that separates North from South. The Marines facing them were spread thin. The first enemy move came
not through the DMZ but around the U.S. left end—the better
part of a North Vietnamese division circling through Laos via
the Ho Chi Minh trail. At Khe Sanh, spotting strategic sim-
ilarities to their greatest victory—against the French in 1954 at
Dienbienphu—North Vietnamese commanders took advantage
of monsoon weather to fortify the heights. From here, they
hoped to wipe out the defenders in the valley, clearing the way
for a drive at the provincial capital of Quang Tri. The French
had lacked air power and reserves; the U.S., which had both,
didn't wait to be shelled. The Marines airlifted in a mobile
reserve and attacked. Their tactic was to use troops to draw fire
and reveal targets, then, as one Marine described it, "step back
and knock the tops off the hills" with 1,300 tons of bombs and
19,000 shells. The well-disciplined North Vietnamese regulars,
using Chinese-made rifles with sniper scopes, at first held their
own. But the bombs took a frightful toll: 764 were known dead,
unknown numbers wounded, and the rest were driven off the
heights.

—"Up Hill 881 with the Marines," Life magazine, May 19, 1967.

[T]here is no question that the big-unit war has been running
strongly in our favor. In the past year and a half our only clearcut defeat was the overrunning of one Special Forces camp. . . .
Within the past year allied forces have inflicted casualties on
the V.C. and N.V.A. in a ratio of at least 6 to 1, by the most
conservative reckoning.

Against the best people in the business, the Americans have

become formidable jungle and counterguerrilla fighters. The performance is all the more remarkable when it is remembered that some of our units have already experienced one complete turnover of personnel, because of the one-year rotation policy, and some are about to experience their second full turnover. That this phasing-in of green troops has gone so smoothly is a tribute to some unsung, unglamorous military training camps in the U.S., now staffed with many a sergeant and captain back from Vietnam. . . . A leathery colonel in the Delta, Charles Murray, himself a Medal of Honor winner from World War II, now commanding a brigade made up almost entirely of draftees, says they are better soldiers than in World War II or Korea, "bigger, physically stronger, faster learners." There is no doubt that the one-year rotation has been a great morale-fortifier and sanity-saver . . . The war will be over, goes one definition, when the V.C. are no more than "a very bad police problem." By that test, V-VN [Victory in Vietnam] Day is probably off somewhere in the early 1970s.

—Hedley Donovan, "Vietnam: Slow, Tough But Coming Along," Life magazine, June 2, 1967.

Progress, in American terms, has been spectacular—enemy killed, bases built, roads cleared, tonnages delivered. American generals debate whether any more troops would be useful;

. . . **June 22, 1967.** A company of the 173rd Airborne Brigade is ambushed near Dakto and suffers heavy casualties. . . **July 2, 1967.** Heavy fighting breaks out near Conthien after North Vietnamese ambush a U.S. Marine platoon. . . **July 7–12, 1967.** Secretary of Defense Robert McNamara goes to South Vietnam for discussions with General Westmoreland about troop increases; they agree on a 55,000-man increase in the coming year. . . **July 10–11, 1967.** Heavy fighting breaks out in Central Highlands near Dakto and Ducco. . . **July 13, 1967.** 12 Americans are killed in Communist shelling of Da Nang air base. . . **September 1, 1967.** Renewed North Vietnamese attacks on U.S. Marine base at Conthien . . . .

Westmoreland says yes, and makes a convincing case; other generals say they literally have run out of stand-up targets. Yet all agree that never has any army performed better in the field than the American forces in Vietnam. All that valor and technique can offer is being delivered. Our troops can move anywhere, occupy just about any place. We can do almost anything we want in this country—except govern. . . . The range of choice this election offers is limited. There is the military ticket—and then come all the others. General Nguyen Van Thieu and Nguyen Cao Ky are the uneasy partners who head the military ticket—and both only four years ago were junior colonels, chart flippers and table setters for their seniors. . . . It would be unfair to dismiss the military ticket as unfit because of their uniforms. Years of war against Communism have taught them an inescapable lesson; unless they get the people actively with them, then they are doomed . . . Only if this new government demonstrates that capacity will the American people next year in *their* election face the the hardest question of all— whether they want to stay the course for what may become the longest war in American history.

> —*Theodore H. White, "Bell of Decision Rings Out in Vietnam," Life magazine, September 1, 1967.*

Over Hanoi, a blast of ack-ack finds its mark and the pilot ejects. Another plane loses a duel with a MiG and its pilot hits the silk . . . In two and a half years 950 U.S. airmen have been

---

. . . **September 3, 1967.** Nguyen Van Thieu is elected President of South Vietnam, and Nguyen Cao Ky is elected Vice-President; opposition candidates charge that the election was rigged. . . **October 13, 1967.** U.S. Marine base at Conthien again comes under North Vietnamese attack . . . .

shot down over the North. Roughly a third of these have been rescued. Another 100 were observed to have gone down with their planes. Of the others, at least 135 and perhaps several hundred more . . . have been interned. . . . Early this year one captured U.S. flier, Lt. Commander Richard Stratton, was put on display at a Hanoi press conference and "confessed" his "crimes." But the intended propaganda effect of this zombie-like performance backfired and Hanoi was charged in many quarters with brainwashing. . . . When the North Vietnamese allowed photographs to be taken showing Lt. Commander Stratton bowing like a robot at a Hanoi "press conference," Americans reacted with shock and dismay at this seeming evidence of brainwashing. "That was a bad day," recalls Alice Stratton, the flier's wife. "It was horrible." It is all that she will permit herself to say on the subject . . .

Brushing aside her own worries, she speaks with compassion of those whose men are listed as missing. "That takes real courage," she says, "going day to day and not even knowing that there's a warm body over there."

. . . Coping with her three young sons helps fill her days. "I don't have time to think," she says, obviously grateful to have it that way. "It really isn't a problem with me." Her youngest son, who is almost 2, doesn't remember his father, but his brothers, 4 and 6, often talk about Daddy. Patrick, the 6-year-old, frequently asks when the war will be over so that his father can come home.

—"U.S. Prisoners in North Vietnam," Life magazine, October 20, 1967.

. . . **October 21, 1967.** 100,000 antiwar protesters march on the Pentagon. . . **October 29, 1967.** U.S. Special Forces camp at Locninh attacked by Vietcong, but attackers are repulsed with heavy casualties. . . **November 3, 1967.** Fighting breaks out near Dakto in Central Highlands, and will continue through most of November with heavy U.S. and North Vietnamese casualties. . . . .

I would like to give you today a short progress report on some aspects of the war in Vietnam, because we in Vietnam are keenly aware of the genuine concern being expressed at home about the complex situation in that country.

The war in Vietnam eludes any precise numerical system of measurement or any easy portrayal of progress on battle maps. The war is unique and complicated in origin, in diversity of form, and its diffusion throughout Vietnam. It is a war which probably could not have occurred in this pattern in any other country in these times. But, if we had not met it squarely, it well could have been the precedent for countless future wars of a similar nature. . . .

I have been observing the war in South Vietnam at close hand for almost four years. . . . I am absolutely certain that whereas in 1965 the enemy was winning, today he is certainly losing. . . .

I see progress as I travel all over Vietnam.

I see it in the attitudes of the Vietnamese.

I see it in the open roads and canals.

I see it in the new crops and the new purchasing power for the farmer.

. . . It lies within our grasp—the enemy's hopes are bankrupt. With your support we will give you a success that will impact not only on South Vietnam, but on every emerging nation in the world.

—*General William C. Westmoreland, speech to the National Press Club, Washington, D.C., November 21, 1967.*

. . . **November 11, 1967.** Vietcong release 3 U.S. POWs in Phnompenh, Cambodia . . . **November 29, 1967.** Robert McNamara, harboring secret doubts about the war in Vietnam, resigns as Secretary of Defense. . . **November 30, 1967.** U.S. Senator Eugene McCarthy, an opponent of the war in Vietnam, announces he will challenge President Johnson for the Democratic presidential nomination in 1968 . . . .

The stark ridge lines studded with shell-splintered tree trunks are the site of the longest and bloodiest single battle of the Vietnam war. The fighting began a month ago after 6,000 North Vietnamese troops—protecting infiltration routes along the Cambodian border—moved into the hills overlooking the U.S. airstrip and Special Forces camp at Dak To. Under attack from 15,000 U.S. and South Vietnamese troops, the bulk of the enemy withdrew into the jungle. But last week, on Hill 875, a tough and disciplined force of North Vietnamese took a stand. Holed up in deep bunkers that defied constant air and artillery attacks, they pinned down a battalion of the U.S. 173rd Airborne Brigade with such fire that for three days the paratroopers could not even evacuate their wounded by helicopter. Finally, behind flamethrowers, reinforcing battalions clawed their way up Hill 854 and took it. The cost: 178 wounded and 79 dead paratroopers—30 of them victims of a misplaced U.S. bomb. Dak To as a whole had claimed at least 273 Americans, 32 South Vietnamese and 1,290 North Vietnamese, a toll exceeding that of the fight for the Ia Drang Valley in November 1965. General William Westmoreland, in Washington for meetings with the President, called Dak To the start of "a great defeat for the enemy."

—*"Victory on a Shattered Ridge,"* Life *magazine, December 1, 1967.*

DECEMBER 31, 1967:

U.S. Troop Level in South Vietnam—485,600
Total U.S. Killed in Vietnam War—19,562

CHAPTER
4

NINETEEN SIXTY-EIGHT proved to be the critical turning point in the war in Vietnam. During the Tet holiday at the end of January, the Communists launched simultaneous assaults on cities and military bases across South Vietnam. The breadth and violence of the attacks were unprecedented. A Viet Cong squad even penetrated the compound of the American embassy in Saigon. Meanwhile a U.S. Marine garrison at an isolated base in Khe Sanh came under protracted siege from North Vietnamese forces, raising the specter of another Dienbienphu.

Americans at home reacted with dismay, having been re-assured so many times in the recent past by their political and military leaders that the "light at the end of the tunnel" was approaching in Vietnam. The shock of the Tet Offensive had dramatic political consequences. Lyndon Johnson was nearly defeated by anti-war challenger Eugene McCarthy in the New Hampshire Democratic primary. Robert Kennedy entered the race for the Democratic nomination soon afterward. At the end of March Lyndon Johnson announced a halt to American bombing of North Vietnam except for an area bordering the Demilitarized Zone (DMZ) separating the two Vietnams. He also announced that he would not be a candidate for re-election in the fall.

Protests against the war continued on college campuses and in the streets, culminating in bloody confrontations with the police in the streets of Chicago at the Democratic National Convention in August. The Democrats chose Hubert Humphrey as their standard bearer; Richard Nixon was the Republican candidate. Nixon declared that he had a "secret plan" to end the war, and in November he won a narrow victory over Humphrey. The war continued to exact heavy casualties, even as the two sides prepared to meet in Paris to begin peace negotiations.

1968: YEAR OF DECISION

This Spring far outshines the previous
*   Springs*
Of victories throughout the land come
*   happy tidings.*
Let South and North emulate each other
*   in fighting the U.S. aggressors!*
Forward!
Total victory shall be ours.

—Poem by Ho Chi Minh, broadcast over Hanoi Radio, January 1,
1968.

0300: BOQ [Bachelor Officers' Quarters] No. 3 reports en-
       emy action
0315: U.S. Embassy under attack

January 21, 1968. North Vietnamese siege of Khe Sanh begins, raising fears of another
Dienbienphu. . . **January 30, 1968.** Viet Cong and North Vietnamese launch Tet Offensive,
with coordinated assaults on cities, provincial capitals, and military bases across South
Vietnam, including the seizure of a portion of the American embassy in Saigon by a Viet
Cong squad . . . .

117

0316: Explosion at Phoenix City BOQ

0317: Explosion at Townhouse BOQ

0318: BOQ No. 1 under attack

0319: MacArthur BOQ under attack

0321: Report of hostile attack at Rex BOQ

0325: Explosion at BOQ No. 2

0340: Automatic weapons fire and attack at BOQ No. 3

0341: MPs at U.S. Embassy request urgent ammo resupply

0342: Heavy sniper fire at Metropole BEQ [Bachelor Enlisted Quarters]

0350: Incoming mortars at Montana BOQ

0358: Saigon port area reports small-arms and automatic weapons fire

0359: Mortars and rockets fired at U.S. Embassy; reinforcements requested

—Log of 716th Military Police Battalion Headquarters, January 31, 1968.

SAIGON (AP)—The Viet Cong shelled Saigon Wednesday in a bold followup of their attacks on eight major cities around the country.

Simultaneously, a suicide squad of guerrilla commandos infiltrated the capital and at least three are reported to have entered the grounds of the new U.S. Embassy near the heart of the city.

U.S. Marine guards at the Embassy, opened only late last year, engaged the infiltrators in an exchange of fire.

—Associated Press wire bulletin, January 31, 1968.

In Memory of
The brave men who died
January 31, 1968,
defending this embassy against
the Viet Cong

Sp4 Charles L. Daniel MPC
Cpl James C. Marshall USMC
Sp4 Owen E. Mebust MPC
Pfc William E. Sebast MPC
Sgt Jonnie B. Thomas MPC

—Plaque in the lobby of the United States Embassy, Saigon

What the hell is going on? I thought we were winning the war!

—CBS Evening News anchorman Walter Cronkite on hearing the news from Saigon, January 31, 1968.

Khe Sanh is a very important tactical and strategic locality. It is the western anchor of our defense line along the Demilitarized Zone in South Vietnam . . . Some days ago the President asked me to have the Joint Chiefs of Staff review the situation at Khe Sanh and provide him with our advice. We did so after having consulted with General Westmoreland . . . We confirmed that General Westmoreland's assessment of the situation was correct and that Khe Sanh can be and should be defended.

—General Earle Wheeler, Chairman of Joint Chiefs of Staff, February 5, 1968.

LITTLE BIG HORN, Dakota, June 27, 1876—Gen. George Armstrong Custer said today in an exclusive interview with this correspondent that the battle of the Little Big Horn had just turned the corner and he could now see the light at the end of the tunnel.

"We have the Sioux on the run," Gen. Custer told me. "Of course, we still have some cleaning up to do, but the Redskins are hurting badly and it will only be a matter of time before they give in."

—*Art Buchwald,* Washington Post, *February 6, 1968.*

It became necessary to destroy the town to save it.

—*[Unidentified U.S. Major, describing the battle to drive the enemy out of Ben Tre in Kien Hoa Province], "Survivors Hunt Dead of Bentre, Turned to Rubble in Allied Raids,"* New York Times, *February 8, 1968.*

SAIGON, South Vietnam, Feb. 7—The American-led camp at Langvei, near the heavily defended United States Marine stronghold of Khesanh, fell today after it had been assaulted by Soviet-made tanks.

South Vietnamese military headquarters reported that 316 allied defenders, including 8 Americans, had been killed or wounded or were missing, and that 76, including 12 Americans, had escaped to Khesanh, according to the Associated Press.

The enemy attacked the Khesanh base with more than 300 artillery, mortar and rocket rounds Thursday, the news agency said. A ground assault on a nearby outpost was repulsed.

—*Charles Mohr, "Allied Post Falls to Tank Assault Near Buffer Zone,"* New York Times, *February 8, 1968.*

It was about this time that copies of the little red British paperback edition of Jules Roy's *The Battle of Dienbienphu* began appearing wherever members of the Vietnam press corps gathered. You'd spot them around the terrace bar of the Continental Hotel, in L'Amiral Restaurant and Aterbea, at the 8th Aerial Port of Tan Son Nhut, in the Marine-operated Danang Press Center and in the big briefing room of JUSPAO in Saigon, where every afternoon at 4:45 spokesmen conducted the daily war briefing which was colloquially referred to as the Five O'Clock Follies, an Orwellian grope through the day's events as seen by the Mission. (It was very hard line.) Those who could find copies were reading Bernard Fall's Dien Bien Phu book, *Hell in a Very Small Place*, which many considered the better book, stronger on tactics, more businesslike, with none of the high-level staff gossip that made the Roy book so dramatic. And as the first Marine briefings on Khe Sanh took place in Marine headquarters at Danang or Dong Ha, the name Dien Bien Phu insinuated itself like some tasteless ghost hawking bad news.

—*Michael Herr,* Dispatches *(1978).*

KHE SANH, Vietnam (AP)—The first shell-burst caught the Marines outside the bunkers filling sandbags. More exploding rockets sent showers of hot fragments zinging. The Americans dove for cover.

"Corpsman! Corpsman!"

The shout came from off to the right.

"We've got wounded here."

"Corpsman! Corpsman!" The shouts now came from the distance. You could see the men dragging a bleeding buddy toward cover.

Inside the bunkers the Marines hugged their legs and bowed their heads, unconsciously trying to make themselves as small as possible. The tempo for the shelling increased and the small opening to the bunker seemed in their minds to grow to the size of a barn door. The 5,000 sandbags around and over the bunker seemed wafer thin. . . .

Outside the random explosions sent thousands of pounds of shrapnel tearing into sandbags and battering already damaged mess halls and tent areas long ago destroyed and abandoned for a life of fear and filth underground.

This is the life in the "V ring," a sharpshooter's term for the inner part of the bull's-eye. At Khe Sanh the "V" ring for the North Vietnamese gunners neatly covers the bunkers of Bravo Company, 3rd Reconnaissance Battalion. In three weeks, more than half the company had been killed or wounded. . . .

In between shellings, Lance Cpl. Richard Noyes, 19, of Cincinnati, Ohio, roughhoused on the dirt floor of his bunker with a friend. Noyes lives with five buddies in the center of the "V" ring. The war was pushed far into the background for a moment as ripples of laughter broke from the tangled, wrestling forms . . .

At night the men in Noyes's bunker sit and talk, sing, play cards, almost anything to keep from being alone with their thoughts. During a night when more than 1,000 rounds hit Khe Sanh, Noyes turned to a buddy and said: "Man, it'll be really decent to go home and never hear words like incoming shells, mortars, rifles, and all that stuff. And the first guy who asks me how it feels to kill, I'll . . ." A pause. Then: "You know, my brother wants me to go duck hunting when I get home. Man, I don't want to even see a slingshot when I get out of here." . . .

Still later, he called out, "Okay, we're going to sing now.

Anyone who can't sing has to hum. Because I said so. Okay, let's hear it."

Lance Cpl. Richard Morris, 24, of North Hollywood, California, began playing a guitar. Two favorites that night were "Five Hundred Miles" and "Where Have All the Flowers Gone?"

A hard emphasis accompanied the verse that went: "Where have all the soldiers gone? To the graveyard every one. When will they ever learn? When will they ever learn?"

Finally the two small naked light bulbs were turned out and the Marines struggled toward sleep.

—*John T. Wheeler, "Life in the V Ring," Associated Press, February 12, 1968.*

A chill, gray mist hangs over the jungled hills around Khe Sanh and drifts down onto the base's metal runway. The morning mist often lasts into the afternoon, the bright sun of recent weeks is lost in monsoonal overcast, and the air is raw and wet with winter. The camp seems to have settled into a dull, lethargic pace to match the dull, damp weather that envelops it. In a mood of resignation, Marines go about their life-or-death work, digging into the red clay, filling sandbags, bolstering the bunkers they know are their one protection against the real rain: the whining rockets and the mortars that come with no warning—just the awful cracking sound as they explode.

The dash for cover is part of every man's routine. "It's a *modus vivendi*," says Protestant Chaplain Ray Stubbe, 29. "The men run for shelter, but they don't cringe when they get there." Except for an occasional case of what the corpsmen call "acute environmental reaction" (shell shock), the Marines at Khe Sanh are taking their ordeal with considerable composure. . . .

The top Marine at Khe Sanh is Col. David E. Lownds, 47, the

mustachioed commander of the 26th Marine Regiment, who oversees the defense of the base from an underground bunker left over by its original French occupants. Sitting in a faded lawn chair, he seldom rests, night or day. He keeps constant watch over the nerve center, a labyrinth of whitewashed rooms lit by bare bulbs and bustling with staff officers and enlisted aides. Is he worried about the huge enemy concentration surrounding him? "Hell no," says Lownds. "I've got Marines. My confidence isn't shaken a bit." He fully recognizes his stand-and-fight mission: "My job is to stay here. My job is to hold. I don't plan on reinforcements." . . .

Most Marines at Khe Sanh feel more than ready for the battle they know they are there for, but they are becoming impatient. The waiting is wearying and frustrating, as day by day they undergo incoming, see friends wounded and killed (total casualties equal 10 percent of the base's men), and remain unable to fight back. "I wish they'd come and get it over with," said Pfc. Larry Jenkins, 18. Despite their perilous position, Jenkins and his comrades at Khe Sanh are spoiling for a fight.

—Don Sider, "Khe Sanh: Ready To Fight," Time magazine, February 16, 1968.

SAIGON, South Vietnam, Feb. 24—The United States Mission conceded today for the first time that the allied effort to pacify the countryside had suffered a "considerable setback" as a result of the Vietcong offensive.

"There has been a loss of momentum, there has been some withdrawal (of security troops) from the countryside, there has been a significant psychological setback both on the part of pacification people themselves and the local population," said a high official of the Mission.

The pacification effort, which seeks to win the allegiance of South Vietnam's peasants, has been regarded here as having the same importance as the military drive.

> —*Bernard Weinraub, "U.S. Admits Blow to Pacification," New York Times, February 25, 1968.*

SAIGON (AP)—Gen. William C. Westmoreland expressed doubt Sunday that North Vietnam could stand a long war. But he said communist forces could strike again and more U.S. troops probably will be required in the war.

The four-star commander of U.S. forces in Vietnam compared the recent communist Lunar New Year offensive to the Battle of the Bulge in World War II, the last major German drive in the conflict.

Westmoreland said:

"I liken the recent Tet offensive by the leadership in Hanoi to the Battle of the Bulge in World War II. By committing a large share of his communist forces to a major offensive, he achieved some tactical surprise. This offensive has required us to react and to modify our plans in order to take advantage of the opportunity to inflict heavy casualties upon him.

"Although the enemy has achieved some temporary psychological advantage, he suffered a military defeat."

> —*Associated Press dispatch, February 25, 1968.*

. . . It seems now more than ever that the bloody experience of Vietnam is to end in a stalemate. This summer's almost certain standoff will either end in real give-and-take negotiations or terrible escalation; and for every means we have to escalate, the enemy can match us, and that applies to invasion of the North, the use of nuclear weapons, or the mere commitment of one hundred or two hundred or three hundred thousand more American troops to the battle. And with each escalation, the world comes close to the brink of cosmic disaster.

To say that we are closer to victory today is to believe, in the face of the evidence, the optimists who have been wrong in the past. To suggest we are on the edge of defeat is to yield to unreasonable pessimism. To say that we are mired in stalemate seems the only realistic, yet unsatisfactory, conclusion.

On the off-chance that military and political analysts are right, in the next months we must test the enemy's intentions in case this is indeed his last big gasp before negotiations. But it is increasingly clear to this reporter that the only rational way out then will be to negotiate, not as victors but as an honorable people who lived up to their pledge to defend democracy, and did the best they could.

This is Walter Cronkite. Good night.

> —*Walter Cronkite's concluding remarks, CBS News Special, "Report from Vietnam," February 27, 1968.*

Just your impression, do you think the U.S. and its allies are losing ground in Vietnam, standing still, or making progress?

	Nov. 1967	*Feb. 1968*
Losing	8%	23%
Standing still	33	38
Making progress	50	33
No opinion	9	6

> —*Gallup Poll of U.S. public opinion, November 1967, February 1968.*

WESTMORELAND REQUESTS 206,000 MORE MEN, STIRRING DEBATE IN ADMINISTRATION

Force Now 510,000

Some in Defense and State Departments Oppose Increase

WASHINGTON, March 9—Gen. William C. Westmoreland has asked for 206,000 more American troops for Vietnam, and the request has touched off a divisive internal debate within high levels of the Johnson Administration.

—Lead story in Sunday New York Times, *March 10, 1968.*

NASHUA, N.H., March 10—Richard M. Nixon will stand firm on his pledge that a new Administration would "end the war" in Vietnam but he will continue to resist pressure from friends and critics alike to explain in detail how he or any other Republican President could achieve that objective.

—Robert B. Semple, Jr., "Nixon Withholds His Peace Ideas," New York Times, *March 11, 1968.*

WASHINGTON, March 10—An Army officer who tried today to picket the White House to protest the Vietnam war was carried away by the Armed Forces Police.

The officer identified himself as Second Lieut. Dennis J. Morrisseau, 25 years old, of Burlington, Vt., stationed at Fort Devens in Massachusetts. He said he was under orders to go to

. . . March 12, 1968. Eugene McCarthy wins 42% of vote in New Hampshire's Democratic primary . . . .

Vietnam soon and did not want to because he objected to the war.

He walked along the sidewalk on the Pennsylvania Avenue side of the Presidential mansion for a few minutes, carrying a hand-painted sign that said, "120,000 American Casualties— Why?" . . .

The Park Police called the Armed Forces Police, which maintains interservice squads of military policemen to patrol the Washington area. Two cars arrived and the officer was taken away for questioning.

> —"White House Police Stop Army Officer Protesting the War, New York Times, March 11, 1968.

CONCORD, N.H., March 12—President Johnson turned back a strong challenge by Senator Eugene J. McCarthy in the first 1968 Democratic primary tonight, but not before the Minnesotan had won about 40 per cent of the vote.

> —Warren Weaver, Jr., "McCarthy Gets About 40%, Johnson and Nixon on Top in New Hampshire Voting," New York Times, March 13, 1968.

People have remarked that this campaign has brought young people back into the system. But it's the other way around. The young people have brought this country back into the system.

> —Senator Eugene McCarthy, victory speech to supporters, March 12, 1968.

Mr. McCarthy's strong showing against President Johnson . . . demonstrated that there is a strong potential in the antiwar movement, and in opposition to President Johnson. . . . For

Senator McCarthy and hundreds of college-age boys and girls who had flocked into this state to aid his campaign, it was a day of triumph only a little short of their wildest expectations. . . . Johnson's supporters, including Governor John W. King and Senator Thomas J. McIntyre, had repeatedly suggested during the campaign that supporting Mr. McCarthy would give aid and comfort to the Communist government in Hanoi.

—*Tom Wicker, "Effects of Primary," New York Times, March 13, 1968.*

When all the parts are added up, the dimension of South Vietnam's losses since Tet become clear: 14,300 civilians dead, 24,000 wounded, 72,000 houses destroyed, 627,000 new refugees. Of the 35 cities hit, 10 suffered major damage: Kontum, Pleiku, Ban Me Thuot, My Tho, Ben Tre, Vinh Long, Chau Doc, Can Tho, Saigon, and Hue. CORDS [Civilian Operations and Revolutionary Development Support] officials estimate that 13 of the country's 44 provinces were so badly hit that pacification has been set back to where it stood at the beginning of 1967. In an additional 16 provinces, it will take three to six months to get the program working again. Only 60 percent of the Revolutionary Development workers have so far been reported at their posts. And, even when nearly all the pacification workers are back on the job, it will be a different kind of job for quite a while: rebuilding the ruins of Tet rather than nation-building for the future.

—*"After 'Tet': Measuring and Repairing the Damage," Time magazine, March 15, 1968.*

PROVIDENCE, R.I., March 15—Vice President Humphrey predicted tonight that despite rifts within the party, Democrats would unite behind President Johnson for re-election . . . Democrats "talk a lot," he said.

"We love ideas. We enjoy debate. But when it comes to the critical issue of advance or retreat, Democrats stand united."

— *"Humphrey Predicts Johnson's Election,"* New York Times, *March 16, 1968.*

WASHINGTON, March 16—Senator Robert F. Kennedy of New York said today that he would seek the Democratic Presidential nomination because the nation's "disastrous, divisive policies" in Vietnam and at home could be changed "only by changing the men who are now making them."

. . . Mr. Kennedy emphasized the war in Vietnam—although in a jab at Richard M. Nixon, considered the leading Republican candidate, he said he could not promise to end it. Mr. Nixon has "pledged" to do so.

Mr. Kennedy said, rather, that he would stop the bombing of North Vietnam, require a greater war effort by South Vietnam, and negotiate with the National Liberation Front, which he said would have to have a place in the future "political process" of South Vietnam.

— *Tom Wicker, "Kennedy to Make 3 Primary Races; Attacks Johnson,"* New York Times, *March 17, 1968.*

COMPANY C, 1ST BATTALION, 20TH INFANTRY: ACTIONS ON 16 AND 17 MARCH 1968 . . . Members of the 2d Platoon began killing Vietnamese inhabitants of My Lai (4) as

---

. . . **March 16, 1968.** Between 200 and 500 South Vietnamese civilians are murdered by members of the Americal Division under the command of Lt. William Calley in what will later become known as the My Lai Massacre . . . .

soon as they entered its western edge. The evidence available indicates they neither sought to take nor did they retain any prisoners, suspects, or detainees while in My Lai (4). As they advanced and discovered homemade bunkers or bomb shelters, many of the soldiers yelled "Lai Day" (the Vietnamese word for "come here"). Failing any response from the Vietnamese inside the bunkers, the soldiers tossed fragmentation grenades into the bunkers, and followed up by spraying the inside with small arms fire. Many witnesses also testified that when Vietnamese did respond most of them were shot down as they exited the bunkers. In at least three instances inside the village, Vietnamese of all ages were rounded up in groups of 5–10 and were shot down. Other inhabitants were shot down while attempting to escape. Women and children, many of whom were small babies, were killed sitting or hiding inside their homes. At least two rapes were participated in and observed by members of the platoon . . . A precise determination of the number of Vietnamese killed by the 2d Platoon is virtually impossible. However, the preponderance of the evidence indicates that at least 50 and perhaps as many as 100 inhabitants, comprised almost exclusively of old men, women, children, and babies, were killed by members of the 2d Platoon while they were in My Lai . . . Based exclusively on the testimony of U.S. personnel who participated in or observed the actions in and around My Lai (4) on 16 March, it is evident that by the time C Company was prepared to depart the area, its members had killed no less than 175–200 Vietnamese men, women, and children . . . There is no substantive evidence to indicate that the company received any enemy fire or any other form of resistance during its movement through the area.

—*Excerpt from the Peers Commission Report (headed by Lt. Gen. W.R. Peers, U.S. Army) on the My Lai Massacre, submitted March 14, 1970.*

One further incident stood out in many GIs' minds: seconds after the shooting stopped, a bloodied but unhurt two-year-old boy miraculously crawled out of the ditch, crying. He began running toward the hamlet. Someone hollered, "There's a kid." There was a long pause. Then [Lt. William] Calley ran back, grabbed the child, threw him back in the ditch and shot him.

—*Seymour Hersh,* My Lai 4: A Report on the Massacre and Its Aftermath *(1970).*

Now that the weather is clearing, jet fighter-bombers roar overhead most of the day, plastering the ridges with napalm that burns off the scrub trees and elephant grass where the NVA [North Vietnamese Army] are dug in. But somehow the enemy troops seem to survive, and during the day they can be seen moving through their trenches. For weeks, one North Vietnamese, armed with a .50-caliber machine gun and known to the Marines as "Luke the Good," has been ripping off his deadly bursts at low-flying aircraft from a foxhole barely 100 yards outside the lines. No amount of napalm has been able to burn Luke out.

—*Merton Perry, "The Dusty Agony of Khe Sanh,"* Newsweek, *March 18, 1968.*

Good evening, my fellow Americans:

Tonight I want to speak to you of peace in Vietnam and Southeast Asia. No other question so preoccupies our people. No other dream so absorbs the 250 million human beings who

. . . **March 31, 1968.** Lyndon Johnson announces steps to de-escalate war in Vietnam, including an end to bombing over most of North Vietnam; he also declares that he will not be a candidate for re-election in 1968 . . . .

live in that part of the world. No other goal motivates American policy in Southeast Asia. . . .

We are prepared to move immediately toward peace through negotiations. So tonight, in the hope that this action will lead to early talks, I am taking the first step to de-escalate the conflict. We are reducing—substantially reducing—the present level of hostilities, and we are doing so unilaterally and at once.

Tonight, I have ordered our aircraft and our naval vessels to make no attacks on North Vietnam, except in the area north of the Demilitarized Zone where the continuing enemy buildup directly threatens allied forward positions and where the movements of their troops and supplies are closely related to that threat. . . .

With America's sons in the fields far away, with America's future under challenge right here at home, with our hopes and the world's hopes for peace in the balance every day, I do not believe that I should devote an hour or a day of my time to any personal partisan causes or to any duties other than the awesome duties of this office—the Presidency of your country.

Accordingly I shall not seek, and I will not accept, the nomination of my party for another term as your President.

—President Lyndon B. Johnson, televised address to the nation, March 31, 1968.

Men who have participated in a decision develop a stake in that decision. As they participate in further, related decisions, their stake increases. It might have been possible to dissuade a man of strong self-confidence at an early stage of the ladder of decision; but it is infinitely harder at later stages since a change

. . . **April 3, 1968.** Hanoi signals its willingness to enter into peace negotiations . . . .

of mind there usually involves implicit or explicit repudiation of a chain of previous decisions. To put it bluntly: at the heart of the Vietnam calamity is a group of able, dedicated men who have been regularly and repeatedly wrong—and whose standing with their contemporaries, and, more important, with history, depends, as they see it, on being proven right. These are not men who can be asked to extricate themselves from error.

—James C. Thomson, Jr., "How Could Vietnam Happen?" Atlantic Monthly, April 1968.

Well, I don't know what will happen now. We've got some difficult days ahead. But it really doesn't matter with me now, because I've been to the mountaintop. And I don't mind. Like anybody, I would like to live a long life. Longevity has its place. But I'm not concerned about that now. I just want to do God's will. And He's allowed me to go up to the mountain, and I've looked over, and I've seen the promised land. I may not get there with you. But I want you to know tonight, that we, as a people will get to the promised land. And so I'm happy tonight. I'm not worried about anything. I'm not fearing any man. Mine eyes have seen the glory of the coming of the Lord.

—Dr. Martin Luther King, Jr., speech in Memphis, Tennessee, April 3, 1968.

Martin Luther King dedicated his life to love and justice for his fellow human beings, and he died because of that effort.

In this difficult day, in this difficult time for the United

States, it is perhaps well to ask what kind of a nation we are and what direction we want to move in. For those of you who are black—considering the evidence there evidently is that there were white people who were responsible—you can be filled with bitterness, with hatred, and a desire for revenge. We can move in that direction as a country, in great polarization—black people amongst black, white people amongst white, filled with hatred toward one another.

Or we can make an effort, as Martin Luther King did, to understand and to comprehend, and to replace that violence, that stain of bloodshed that has spread across our land, with an effort to understand with compassion and love. . . . What we need in the United States is not division; what we need in the United States is not hatred; what we need in the United States is not violence or lawlessness, but love and wisdom, and compassion toward one another, and a feeling of justice towards those who still suffer within our country. . . .

—*Senator Robert F. Kennedy, April 4, 1968.*

WASHINGTON, April 5—President Johnson ordered 4,000 regular Army and National Guard troops into the nation's capital tonight to try to end riotous looting, burglarizing and burning by roving bands of Negro youths. The arson and looting began yesterday after the murder of the Rev. Dr. Martin Luther King Jr. in Memphis . . . The National Guard also was called out in a half-dozen other cities in an effort to stem disorders or guard against them—Chicago, Detroit, Boston, Jackson, Miss., Raleigh, N.C., and Tallahassee, Fla.

—*Ben A. Franklin, "Army Troops in Capital As Negroes Riot; Guard Sent into Chicago, Detroit, Boston," New York Times, April 6, 1968.*

KHESANH, South Vietnam, Saturday, April 6—The 76-day North Vietnamese siege of the Marine base at Khesanh was officially declared lifted yesterday.

United States marines and helicopter-borne Army troops today pushed toward what was described as North Vietnamese regimental headquarters south of the base.

The 20,000-man relief column reached the base and then fanned out on three sides in search of the vanishing enemy soldiers.

—*"Siege of Khesanh Declared Lifted; Troops Hunt Foe,"* New York Times, *April 6, 1968.*

More than 200,000 college and high school students in the metropolitan area cut classes yesterday during a student strike against the Vietnam war . . . The mood of most of the demonstrations combined grim determination, high spirits and youthful verve. With the age spread from the mid-20's on college campuses down to 11 and 12 at the junior high schools, the protests took on some of the character of a children's crusade.

A column of 225 junior and senior high school students got a mixed reaction from adults as they paraded up Broadway from 65th to 95th Street chanting "Peace Now" and other slogans.

"They're only 14 or 15 years old; what do they know about the war?" asked Paul Hagan, a 65-year-old Navy veteran who lives at the Nevada Hotel.

"Wonderful, wonderful, God bless them all," said Mrs. Sylvia Weinstein of 1295 Grand Concourse, the Bronx, explaining that she didn't want her 20-year-old grandson or any other boy to be sent to Vietnam.

—*Michael Stern, "200,000 Cut Classes in a War Protest,"* New York Times, *April 27, 1968.*

LOS ANGELES, Thursday, June 6—Senator Robert F. Kennedy, the brother of a murdered President, died at 1:44 A.M. today of an assassin's shots.

The New York Senator was wounded more than 20 hours earlier, moments after he had made his victory statement in the California primary.

> —*Gladwin Hill, "Kennedy Is Dead, Victim of Assassin; Suspect, Arab Immigrant, Arraigned," New York Times, June 6, 1968.*

The sixties came to an end in a Los Angeles hospital on June 6, 1968.

> —*Richard Goodwin, Remembering America: A Voice from the Sixties (1988).*

BOSTON, June 6—A defendant at the Spock conspiracy trial testified today that he believed the Vietnam war was inciting violence in America, and that "nothing could be done about it unless the war is stopped."

Marcus Raskin, a former White House disarmament aide, said he first voiced that opinion early last summer. He said then that the United States was "using violence as a spearhead" and that individual citizens were "taking their cues from the state in the use of violence."

. . . Mr. Raskin, along with Dr. Benjamin Spock, 65 years

. . . **May 3, 1968.** Peace talks between the U.S. and North Vietnam are announced to begin the following week in Paris. . . **May 25, 1968.** The Viet Cong launch a new offensive in Saigon. . . **June 5, 1968.** Senator Robert F. Kennedy is shot after winning the California Democratic primary; he dies the following day. . . . .

old, pediatrician; the Rev. William Sloane Coffin, Sr., 43, Yale University chaplain; Mitchell Goodman, 44, writer and teacher, and Michael K. Ferber, 23 a Harvard graduate student, are charged by the Government with conspiring to aid young men to evade the draft and disrupt induction centers. If convicted they face five years in prison and $10,000 fines.

—*"Spock Trial Told War Spurs Violence,"* New York Times, *June 7, 1968.*

The goal written on the university walls was "Create two, three, many Columbias"; it meant expand the strike so that the U.S. must either change or send its troops to occupy American campuses. . . .

Columbia opened a new tactical stage in the resistance movement which began last fall: from the overnight occupation of buildings to permanent occupation; from the mill-ins to the creation of revolutionary committees; from symbolic civil disobedience to barricaded resistance . . .

In the buildings occupied at Columbia, the students created what they called a "new society" or "liberated area" or "commune," a society in which decent values would be lived out even though university officials might cut short the communes through use of police . . .

We are moving toward power—the power to stop the machine if it cannot be made to serve humane ends . . . The students at Columbia discovered that barricades are only the beginning of what they call "bringing the war home."

—*Tom Hayden, "Two, Three, Many Columbias,"* Ramparts *magazine, June 15, 1968.*

. . . **June 10, 1968.** General Creighton Abrams succeeds William Westmoreland as U.S. Commander, MACV. . . . .

The U.S. last week began to abandon Khe Sanh, the once idyllic valley in South Viet Nam's northwest corner that early this year became the scene of the war's biggest and bitterest siege. The news could hardly have been more startling. For months, the American people had been told that the base was indispensable to U.S. strategy and prestige. When its 6,200-man garrison came under siege and heavy artillery bombardment from the North Vietnamese in mid-January, some observers saw an ominous similarity to Dien-bienphu ... Khe Sanh thus became a symbol—justifiably or not—of U.S. determination to stick it out under heavy pressure.

And yet, scarcely half a year later, the U.S. Marines were out of the base. Amid occasional incoming shellbursts, bulldozers clattered across the base last week, filling the red clay scars that trenches had cut into the once verdant plateau, burying the hulks of crippled aircraft, Jeeps and trucks ... Demolition men destroyed bunker after bunker, the single bit of protection against the rain of North Vietnamese steel that had lashed the base for almost half a year and cost its U.S. Marine defenders 199 dead and 1,600 wounded. . . .

Hanoi gloated that the abandonment of Khe Sanh was a "grave defeat for the United States." The move might be a bitter comment on war and on the way in which a bravely and passionately held position can become irrelevant. But, in fact, the evacuation of the base reflects recognition of changed realities—and a return to the flexibility that has always marked U.S. military tactics.

—"Khe Sanh: Symbol No More," Time *magazine, July 5, 1968.*

. . . **August 26–29, 1968.** Clashes between antiwar protesters and police mar Democratic National Convention in Chicago. . . . .

August 29. It was one of those cool evenings you don't usually get in Chicago this time of year. "You don't often get it nice like this till after Labor Day," the cabdriver had said. The air clear. The night breeze blowing in off the lake. There were boats at anchor in the marina. Dozens of small white boats. White boats floating in the dark water. The boy beside me, a dark-haired boy with a scraggly mustache, was dressed in Levi's and some kind of T-shirt and was called Dave, and blood was running down one side of his face and he was sitting in the gutter holding this girl, and people were screaming, really screaming, and the kids were standing in the middle of the road between the Hilton Hotel and the Blackstone, and then a tight-packed gang of about thirty cops came out of a side street, more or less on the run, holding their clubs out, rushing, pushing into the kids. One kid turned to go by the cops, get out of the way, and one of the cops grabbed the kid by one arm, spinning him off balance, and hit him on the back of the neck with his club. The kid yelled "Hey! God*dam!*" and the cop, who wore a blue helmet and a wide belt, shoved his club hard into the kid's belly, and the kid sort of doubled up, and the cop grabbed him by the arm again and pulled him down the street toward where a white paddy wagon was parked in the middle of the road—one of three paddy wagons, or white armored trucks, with their back doors open. . . . You keep reading in the papers about how "demonstrators" had been "thumped" or "thwacked" with "nightsticks." When you are six feet tall and weigh a hundred and seventy pounds and hit a man on the head with a thick piece of wood—a thick, hard piece of wood—you do not "thump" him. You give him not only hurt, which is finite, but something worse, something degrading, and this may be why the people who now advocate clubbing in our country seem to be the same people who have trouble understanding that the dropping of bombs on other nations is something more, and worse, than the "delivery" of "hardware."

—*Michael J. Arlen, "A Wednesday Evening in Chicago,"* The New Yorker *magazine, September 7, 1968.*

Schism, bitterness, demands for violent solution, disenchantment with the way things are, fear of what may be—these are the forces, some would say the demons, that are loose in the U.S. in 1968. The demons accompanied the Democrats to Chicago. A deeply divided party met amid paroxysms of violence in the city and obsessive security measures that surrounded a major function of U.S. democracy with the air of a police state. A bitter but rational argument about Vietnam was traumatically translated into street battles between protesters and police. Nominees and other speakers spent valuable time condemning or justifying the conduct of Mayor Richard Daley's heavy-handed cops.

The images of Chicago will haunt the Democrats during the campaign. . . .

—*"Survival at the Stockyards,"* Time *magazine, September 6, 1968.*

The Viet Nam war has divided and demoralized the American people as have few other issues in this century. It led, on March 31, to Lyndon Johnson's renunciation of the presidency in the realization that he might well have been defeated for re-

. . . October 31, 1968. President Lyndon Johnson announces end of bombing of North Vietnam in an attempt to spur a breakthrough in Paris Peace Talks; President Thieu opposes move . . . .

election. Its steadily growing cost was perhaps the greatest single obstacle to Johnson's hopes of building a Great Society for the U.S. in its cities, countryside and classrooms. The war's ugliness, and the often misunderstood reasons behind U.S. participation in it, greatly contributed to the rebelliousness of America's young. More than anything else, it has been Hubert Humphrey's identification with the President's war policy that has cost him Democratic and independent support through the election campaign. Thus it came as the supreme irony of the Johnson Administration that, as Americans prepared to go to the polls this week to vote for another President, the agony of Viet Nam appeared about to be alleviated.

In a televised address to the nation that may rate as the high point of his career, the President announced: "I have now ordered that all air, naval and artillery bombardment of North Viet Nam cease," effective twelve hours after he spoke. "What we now expect—what we have a right to expect—are prompt, productive, serious and intensive negotiations." When those negotiations resume in Paris this week, the morning after the U.S. elections, representatives of both the Saigon government and the Viet Cong are expected to take part—though Johnson emphasized that the Communist participation "in no way involves" U.S. recognition of the Viet Cong's political representatives . . . Even with a pause, the war will be far from finished. During negotiations to end the Indo-China War in 1954, the Vietnamese Communists proved their skill at "fighting while talking." They must be expected to do so once more. But the bombing halt, the President suggested, is an acceptable risk . . . the peace negotiations may now move toward a sensible resolution. (A likely first step would be a cease-fire before year's end.) If that should indeed be the result, ending the anguish and self-doubt that have afflicted American society as a result of the conflict, the gamble is one that the U.S. should be eager to underwrite.

> —*"The Bombing Halt: Johnson's Gamble for Peace,"* Time *magazine,*
> *November 8, 1968.*

Had there been a sharp definition of [Humphrey's and Nixon's] views on Vietnam, the war might have provided the great cutting edge of the election. But both candidates seemed engaged in variations of a fugue set by Lyndon Johnson. From beginning to end, Vietnam always rested in every poll, private, public, or scholastic, as the number-one concern of the American people. Except that, on further refinement, no candidate could do anything with the information, for, once Americans had expressed this critical concern, they divided sharply as to how the Vietnam war might be solved. A candidate accepting surrender would have been destroyed; a candidate insisting on conquest at all cost would similarly have been destroyed. Thus both candidates passed on the issue of Vietnam, using it only to shade their self-portraits as men of independent thinking, deep patriotism, and hidden concern.

> —*Theodore H. White,* The Making of the President, 1968 *(1969).*

PRESIDENTIAL ELECTION, 1968:

Candidate	*Party*	*% of Popular Vote*
Richard M. Nixon	Republican	43.4
Hubert M. Humphrey	Democratic	42.7
George C. Wallace	Independent	13.5

. . . **November 6, 1968.** Richard Nixon defeats Hubert Humphrey for U.S. presidency . . . .

I saw many signs in the campaign. Some of them were not friendly and some were very friendly. But the one that touched me the most was the one that I saw in Deshler, Ohio, at the end of a long day of whistle-stopping. . . . A teenager held up a sign, "Bring Us Together." And that will be the great objective of this administration at the outset, to bring the American people together.

—*President-elect Richard M. Nixon, victory speech, November 6, 1968.*

"Rock and Roll music contributes to both the usage of drugs and the high VD rate among the enlisted men in the Army today."

This statement from an Army Captain represents the off-the-record opinion of most high-ranking officers in the Armed Services today. But there is nothing they can do about it.

The Armed Forces have changed dramatically in the last four years. The raising of draft quotas and the tightening of deferment and exemption loopholes has made for a different military, with a higher proportion of men who would otherwise be in college, and a far greater number of men of one generation drafted into the service.

Briefly put, there is a flowering of rock and roll and dope among the unwilling soldiers of today. It is altogether out of hand. It already involves so many men that the brass can't even begin to crack down on it.

"Lots of guys come over here very lame but go home heads. Everyone is excited about trying it 'back in the world' because it is so groovy even at this down place. Guys have mustaches and long sideburns that the average citizen would never believe they were soldiers. We are anxious to get back and grow wild

hair and beards without any restrictions. Beads and Peace symbols are worn with the uniform."—A Corporal in Phu Bai, Vietnam.

In the past year the Army has been directly responsible for turning on probably more than a quarter of a million young American innocents by sending them to Vietnam, and thousands of others merely by putting them together with others of their age—whether in Europe, Asia, or even right home down in Louisiana. But most of all it is Vietnam: the Army has taken hundreds of thousands of students out of school and plopped them into what seems like a marijuana-heaven on earth. In Vietnam, you can buy marijuana already processed into cigarette form, packaged 10 to the pack (200 to the carton) and a pack costs a dollar . . .

Recently some people in the peace movement have been taking an interest in the plight of the large-scale slice of this generation unwillingly imprisoned in olive drab. In addition to the organized pacifists and radicals who put out the GI-oriented newspapers *The Ally, The Bond, Vietnam GI* and others, an organization founded by Fred Gardner of *Ramparts* Magazine (Summer of Support) has been establishing coffeehouses in the vicinity of half a dozen Stateside military bases.

These coffeehouses provide a place to talk and listen to music in an un-military environment. They provide the only taste of freedom and Bohemianism available to the men at the bases, many of which are located in dreary places in the rural South. Tom Cleaver writes about musical tastes at the Oleo Strut, near Camp Hood, Killeen, Texas:

"There is more political content than one would probably find in a civilian community, but I think that this is because of the same reasons that black slaves had political music. It is a quiet way of expressing what they think without being too active about it, thus keeping down the possibility of individual visibility."

Enlisted servicemen make up a lot of people, caught in a particularly nasty and confusing middle-of-things. But it seems plain that it's all one generation, uniformed or not.

—Charles Perry, "Is This Any Way to Run the Army?" Rolling Stone
magazine, November 9, 1968.

DECEMBER 31, 1968:

U.S. Troop Level in South Vietnam—536,000
Total U.S. Killed in Vietnam War—36,151

CHAPTER 5

PRESIDENT RICHARD NIXON intended to end the war in Vietnam, but he did not intend to lose it. In 1969 he announced the new policy of "Vietnamization." American ground forces would be gradually withdrawn from combat, while South Vietnamese forces picked up the burden of fighting the Communists. Meanwhile the U.S. air war was intensified, including the start of the secret bombing of North Vietnamese bases and infiltration routes in neutral Cambodia. Americans casualties dropped from the record levels of 1968, but bloody and seemingly futile battles such as "Hamburger Hill" in May 1969 eroded military morale. The fall of 1969 saw some of the largest antiwar demonstrations of the decade. And when Nixon ordered American troops to cross into Cambodia at the end of April 1970 in an "incursion," he was shaken by the breadth and ferocity of the protests that followed.

Peace talks in Paris dragged on. Americans were sick of the war, and eager to believe that Nixon's policies would bring "peace with honor." Relatively few cared any longer about the ultimate fate of South Vietnam, although many cared passionately about the conditions endured by American POW's in North Vietnam. Antiwar protests continued, and George McGovern won the Democratic nomination for President on an antiwar platform. A new Communist military offensive in the spring of 1972 brought American bombing of Hanoi and Haiphong. Nixon's political position was strengthened by the diplomatic overtures he made to the People's Republic of China and the Soviet Union in 1972. In November, after Secretary of State Henry Kissinger announced that "peace is at hand" in Vietnam, Nixon handily trounced his Democratic challenger.

South Vietnamese president Nguyen Van Thieu opposed any settlement with the Communists that allowed the North Vietnamese to keep their troops in place in South Vietnam. To reassure Thieu of continued American support, Nixon ordered heavy American bombing raids against Hanoi in December. In January the Paris peace accords were signed. With the return of American POW's, and the withdrawal of all but a handful of U.S. military personnel in South Vietnam, the American part of the war was over.

NIXON'S WAR,
1969–1973

The greatest honor history can bestow is the title of peace-maker. This honor now beckons America—the chance to help lead the world at last out of the valley of turmoil and onto that high ground of peace that man has dreamed of since the dawn of civilization. . . .

—*President Richard M. Nixon, inaugural address, January 20, 1969.*

[The] commitment of five hundred thousand Americans has settled the issue of the importance of Vietnam. For what is involved now is confidence in American promises.

—*National Security Adviser Henry Kissinger, "The Vietnam Negotations," Foreign Affairs, January 1969.*

January 16, 1969. Negotiators at Paris Peace Talks agree on expanded talks, including Saigon and Viet Cong. . . **January 20, 1969.** Richard Nixon inaugurated as President of the United States . . . .

I call it the Madman Theory, Bob. I want the North Vietnamese to believe I've reached the point where I might do *anything* to stop the war. We'll just slip the word to them that "for God's sake, you know Nixon is obsessed about Communism. We can't restrain him when he's angry—and he has his hand on the nuclear button"—and Ho Chi Minh himself will be in Paris in two days begging for peace.

> —*Richard Nixon in conversation with H.R. Haldeman [White House aide, 1969–1973], 1969.*

I firmly believe that without the Vietnam War there would have been no Watergate. Without the Vietnam War, Richard Nixon might have had the most successful Presidency since Harry Truman's. With Henry Kissinger as his point man he would have achieved his stunning diplomatic successes in China, the Soviet Union, and the Middle East—and be a President who is revered today.

But the Vietnam War destroyed Nixon as completely as it shattered President Johnson.

> —*H.R. Haldeman, The Ends of Power (1978).*

PARIS, Feb. 13—The opposing sides at the peace talks on Vietnam talked past each other again at their fourth plenary session today. No way out of the present impasse was in sight.

The restatements of earlier proposals and demands, repetitions of old charges, and even occasional invective at the session sounded perfunctory. It lasted 6 hours and 10 minutes.

> —*Paul Hofmann, "Paris Talks Resume; Deadlock Continues," New York Times, February 14, 1969.*

. . . **February 6, 1969.** President Nixon declares there will have to be progress in Paris Peace Talks before U.S. troops begin to be withdrawn. . . **February 23, 1969.** Communist forces launch widespread attacks across South Vietnam in new offensive. . . . .

After many months of relative calm in Viet Nam, the Communists had put the fight back into their "fight and negotiate" formula. All week, Communist rockets and mortars rained down, hitting more than 200 cities, towns and military installations from the Demilitarized Zone to the Delta. Yet Hanoi's post-Tet 1969 offensive was initially hardly comparable to last year's campaign in scope, scale and success. This time the allies knew that an attack was coming almost to the hour, and were prepared . . . Far less damage was done this time in terms of civilian casualties, houses destroyed, and the disruption of allied programs. But military losses—more than 300 U.S. and 700 South Vietnamese dead—were running near the weekly levels of Tet 1968.

—*"A Time of Testing in Viet Nam,"* Time *magazine, March 7, 1969.*

SAIGON, South Vietnam, May 19—American planes and artillery pounded North Vietnamese positions on Apbia, a mountain near the Laotian border, today as United States paratroops rested after 10 futile attempts in nine days to storm the 3,000-foot peak. . . .

The battle, in which 353 North Vietnamese and 39 Americans have been reported killed and 228 Americans wounded, has developed into one of the longest, toughest campaigns of recent months.

Troops of the 101st Airborne Division have made 10 assaults against the enemy's terraced fighting positions. Three times

. . . **March 18, 1969.** Operation Menu, secret U.S. bombing of Cambodia, begins. . . **May 10–20, 1969.** Fighting to drive Communists off Apbia mountain near Laotian border leads to heavy U.S. casualties in what becomes known as the battle of "Hamburger Hill" . . . .

they reached the top, only to be hurled back by small-arms fire and rocket-propelled grenades.

"This is my third war and I haven't bumped into a fight like this since World War II," said Col. Joseph Conmy Jr. of Washington, who commands the division's Third Brigade. "This crowd must have gotten the word from Uncle Ho."

> —"G.I.'s in 10th Try Fail to Rout Foe on Peak at Ashau," New York Times, May 20, 1969.

WASHINGTON, May 20—Senator Edward M. Kennedy, challenging the Nixon Administration's military tactics in Vietnam, charged today that bloody assaults such as those in the battle for Apbia Mountain were "senseless and irresponsible."

In his most pointed criticism to date of the Administration's Vietnam policy, the Massachusetts Democrat declared: "American lives are too valuable to be sacrificed for military pride."

> —Hedrick Smith, "Kennedy Assails Vietnam Tactics," New York Times, May 21, 1969.

Ap Bia Mountain anchors the northwest corner of South Viet Nam's A Shau Valley, since 1966 a major infiltration route for Communist forces from the Ho Chi Minh Trail in Laos to the coastal cities of northern I Corps. It is a mountain much like any other in that part of the Highlands, green, triple-canopied and spiked with thick stands of bamboo. On military maps it is listed as Hill 937, the number representing its height in meters. Last week it acquired another name: Hamburger Hill. It was a

... **May 11–12, 1969.** Communists shell cities across South Vietnam, including Saigon.

grisly but all too appropriate description, for the battle in and around Ap Bia took the lives of 84 G.I.'s and wounded 480 more. Such engagements were familiar enough in Viet Nam up until a year ago. But coming at this stage of the war and the peace talks, the battle for Hamburger Hill set off tremors of controversy that carried all the way to Capitol Hill. . . .

After so many costly failures to gain Ap Bia's summit, some U.S. soldiers were dispirited. "There were lots of people in Bravo Company [which had borne the brunt of the casualties] who were going to refuse to go up again," one soldier said. "There's been low morale, but never before so low—because we felt it was all so senseless."

—*"The Battle for Hamburger Hill,"* Time *magazine, May 30, 1969.*

SAIGON, South Vietnam, June 17—North Vietnamese troops are reported back in force on Apbia Mountain, and a United States general said he was ready to fight for the peak again, "if it takes an entire division."

United States intelligence sources said today that up to 1,000 enemy soldiers had returned to the 3,000-foot mountain. Its capture by United States paratroopers last month cost the lives of 50 American soldiers and more than 600 North Vietnamese, and set off a controversy in Washington . . .

Maj. Gen. John M. Wright, Jr., commander of the 101st Airborne Division, stationed in that area, said in an interview

...**June 8, 1969.** President Nixon and President Thieu meet on Midway Island; Nixon announces withdrawal of 25,000 U.S. troops from South Vietnam by the end of August ...**June 10, 1969.** The Communists announce formation of a "Provisional Revolutionary Government" as a rival to the Saigon government in South Vietnam . . . .

that if it should become necessary to attack again, he was "prepared to commit everything that it takes, up to the entire division, to do the job." But he said there were no present plans for another ground assault on the peak.

—*"Foe Reported Back on Hamburger Hill,"* New York Times, June 18, 1969.

The faces shown on the next pages are the faces of American men killed—in the words of the official announcement of their deaths—"in connection with the conflict in Vietnam." The names, 242 of them, were released by the Pentagon during the week of May 28 through June 3, a span of no special significance except that it includes Memorial Day. The numbers of the dead are average for any seven-day period during this stage of the war.

It is not the intention of this article to speak for the dead. We cannot tell with any precision what they thought of the political currents which drew them across the world. From the letters of some, it is possible to tell they felt strongly that they should be in Vietnam, that they had great sympathy for the Vietnamese people and were appalled at their enormous suffering. Some had voluntarily extended their tours of combat duty; some were desperate to come home. Their families provided most of these photographs, and many expressed their own feelings that their sons and husbands died in a necessary cause. Yet in a time when the numbers of Americans killed in this war—36,000—though far less than the Vietnamese losses, have exceeded the dead in the Korean War, when the nation continues week after week to

. . . **June 23, 1969.** Communists besiege U.S. Special Forces camp at Benhet, near Cambodian and Laotian borders; the siege is broken on July 2 by an ARVN rescue column . . . .

be numbed by a three-digit statistic which is translated to direct anguish in hundreds of homes all over the country, we must pause to look into the faces. More than we must know *how many*, we must know *who*. The faces of one week's dead, unknown but to families and friends, are suddenly recognized by all in this gallery of young American eyes.

— *"Vietnam, One Week's Dead,"* Life *magazine, June 27, 1969.*

It was one month to the day since President Nixon had announced his intention to withdraw 25,000 U.S. troops from Vietnam, and now the first contingent of departing Americans was assembled, to the tune of the Colonel Bogey March, on the steamy tarmac of Saigon's Tan Son Nhut airport. The place was festooned with banners. Pretty South Vietnamese girls in diaphanous *ao dais* held up neatly lettered signs reading FARE-WELL TO THE OLD RELIABLES—a reference to the nickname of the Ninth Infantry Division. And on the reviewing stand, Gen. Creighton Abrams, his sleeves rolled up above his elbows, made a gruff little speech praising the men and assuring them that the day was a "historic occasion."

Abe Abrams was, of course, right. True, the Saigon leave-taking was in no way comparable to those exhilarating days at the end of World Wars I and II when Johnnie—having fought the good fight against a clearly malign enemy—came marching home again to the acclaim of a grateful country. Yet, last week's departure of 814 men of the 3rd Battalion, 60th Infantry, Ninth Division was undeniably freighted with historical significance. For after years of steady escalation—and after more than 36,000 American battlefield deaths—the U.S. had taken its first small step toward disengagement from Vietnam.

— *"Beginning of the End?",* Newsweek, *July 21, 1969.*

It was a display without historical parallel, the largest expression of public dissent ever seen in this country. Across the land the demonstrators gathered, talking, reading names from long lists of war dead, showing the V-sign of peace. As night fell, they moved through the shadows carrying their candles like pilgrims in a cave . . . Vietnam Moratorium Day seemed to have a quality of sweetness about it, a cheerfulness, a suspension of anger and even passion, a decorum surpassing all previous antiwar protests. The country is plainly divided on short-term means and strategy, but the Moratorium demonstrated a kind of public unity of frustration, a vast heaving of the public impatience . . . . In Boston, 100,000 turned out, 30,000 marched past the White House in Washington, there were another 12,000 in Chicago, and in a Kansas college town, a bell tolled every four seconds in honor of the American dead. Hundreds of colleges and high schools closed for the day. A few counterdemonstrations developed, a few stones and angry words were exchanged. But for an outpouring so great, the day was strikingly nonviolent. . . . The effect of the demonstration on national policy and the men who make it cannot truly be known for some time, if indeed it can ever be measured. Neither can its effect on the bulk of Americans and their attitudes on the war. Unquestionably, however, a large number of people not previ-

---

. . . **July 30, 1969.** President Nixon visits South Vietnam, meeting with President Thieu and with U.S. troops. . . **September 3, 1969.** Ho Chi Minh dies at the age of 79. . . **September 5, 1969.** Lt. William Calley is charged with murder of 109 Vietnamese civilians in My Lai in March 1968. . . **September 16, 1969.** President Nixon announces plans for withdrawal of 35,000 Americans from South Vietnam. . . **September 19, 1969.** President Nixon announces reduced draft calls for the remainder of 1969. . . **October 15, 1969.** A million or more Americans nationwide take part in local demonstrations against the war as part of the Vietnam Moratorium . . . .

ously committed to dissent showed themselves, on this day, to be so committed.

> —*"America Gathers Under a Sign of Peace,"* Life *magazine, October 24, 1969.*

The policy of the previous administration not only resulted in our assuming the primary responsibility for fighting the war, but even more significantly did not adequately stress the goal of strengthening the South Vietnamese so that they could defend themselves when we left.

The Vietnamization plan was launched following [Secretary of Defense Melvin] Laird's visit to Vietnam in March. Under this plan, I ordered first a substantial increase in the training and equipment of South Vietnamese forces.

In July, on my visit to Vietnam, I changed General Abrams' orders so that they were consistent with the objectives of our new policies. Under the new orders, the primary mission of our troops is to enable the South Vietnamese forces to assume the full responsibility for the security of South Vietnam. . . .

And now we have begun to see the results of this long overdue change in American policy in Vietnam.

—After 5 years of Americans going into Vietnam, we are finally bringing men home. By December 15, over 60,000 men will have been withdrawn from South Vietnam—including 20 percent of all of our combat forces.

—The South Vietnamese have continued to gain in strength. As a result they have been able to take over combat responsibilities from our American troops. . . .

. . . **November 3, 1969.** President Nixon appeals in television broadcast for the "silent majority" of Americans to support his policies in Vietnam . . . .

And so tonight—to you, the great silent majority of my fellow Americans—I ask for your support. . . . Let us be united for peace. Let us also be united against defeat. Because let us understand: North Vietnam cannot defeat or humiliate the United States. Only Americans can do that. . . . Thank you and good night.

—*President Richard M. Nixon, televised address to the nation, November 3, 1969.*

I doubt that we could have continued fighting the war if we had not been gradually withdrawing our troops. Since 1969, we had been faced with the danger of Congress legislating an end to our involvement. Anti-war senators and congressmen had been introducing resolutions to force us to trade a total withdrawal of our troops for the return of our POWs . . . We were able to prevent the passage of those bills only because our withdrawal announcements provided those whose support for the war was wavering with tangible evidence that our involvement was winding down.

—*Richard M. Nixon,* No More Vietnams *(1985).*

Down Washington's Pennsylvania Avenue, the "path of Presidents," they marched in the morning chill, some 250,000 Americans come to their Capital to tell their President he was wrong. They bore the flags of the United States and the Viet

Cong—and some waved banners hailing Che Guevara. They were led by the men and women who have come to embody the several strains of American protest—Eugene McCarthy, Coretta King, Arlo Guthrie, Benjamin Spock—and by twelve wooden coffins containing the names of U.S. servicemen killed in Vietnam. This was the 1969 March on Washington, the largest anti-war demonstration ever held in the Capital, and to the relief of most and the consternation of a few, it proceeded for the most part in dignity and peace. . . .

If there was a high moment, it came when folk singer Pete Seeger stepped up to the microphone. Sporting a full beard, and accompanied by the rich baritone of his Negro "brother" Fred Kirkpatrick, Seeger brought the mass to its feet with a song called "Bring Them Home." Then, as the crowd chorused, "Give peace a chance," Seeger's voice echoed over the Mall: "Are you listening, Nixon? Are you listening, Agnew?" Scores of thousands of people, their fingers thrust upward in the symbolic "V" gesture, roared their approval.

—*"The Big March: On a Treadmill?"*, Newsweek, November 24, 1969.

PLEIKU, South Vietnam, November 27—More than a hundred G.I.'s serving in a field evacuation hospital here boycotted Thanksgiving dinner today in a quiet 24-hour fast designed as a protest against American involvement in the war here. . . .

Similar fasts on a smaller scale were reported in several scattered units. Except for troops in the field who dined on C-rations, the rest of the 484,000 United States soldiers in South Vietnam ate a traditional dinner of turkey, cornbread dressing, cranberry sauce, sweet potatoes and pumpkin pie.

The fast at this sprawling American base in the red sands of the cool Central Highlands halfway between Saigon and the demilitarized zone was the most notable antiwar activity by G.I.'s in South Vietnam since a handful of soldiers donned black armbands during the moratorium demonstration on Oct. 15.

Out of the 141 soldiers of rank below specialist 5 serving with the 71st Medical Detachment of the 44th Medical Group, only eight appeared for dinner at the mess hall, which was decorated with crepe-paper streamers and a large red "Happy Thanksgiving" sign. . . .

The purpose of the fast was expressed in an open letter to President Nixon written several weeks ago by a loose group of 10 noncareer soldiers.

The letter, circulated on this and some other bases with a space for signatures, said, "Sir: So long as American soldiers continue and fight in a senseless war that cannot be won, we the undersigned feel that we have very little for which to be thankful."

—*Ralph Blumenthal, "100 G.I.'s in Pleiku Fast for Holiday," New York Times, November 28, 1969.*

The image of a dead child flashed upon the screen. In an instant, it clicked off and was replaced by another grisly picture—this one of a young woman lying broken and covered with blood in the mud of her village. As the pictorial inventory of the dead continued, congressmen sitting in the walnut-paneled committee room on Capitol Hill watched in stunned silence. They had come to see Secretary of the Army Stanley Resor present a series of color photographs taken in the village of Song My, where U.S. troops allegedly massacred scores of South Vietnamese civilians more than twenty months ago. And the horror show they witnessed last week had a telling effect. . . . Two weeks after the incident first came to public attention, the harsh reality of Song My suddenly was etched in sharp and repugnant detail. True, it was still unclear precisely how many South Vietnamse civilians had fallen victim to American bullets; figures ranged from 109 to 567. But no one could any longer seriously doubt that a platoon of GI's had, in fact, participated in wanton slaughter. . . .

What made the incident peculiarly painful was that much of the fresh evidence that came to light last week was presented on the nation's television screens by those who had actually been at Song My during the massacre. Reporters struck a particularly rich vein in the person of Paul David Meadlo, 22, a farm boy from Indiana who participated in the attack and who lost a foot in a booby trap the next day. Interviewed on CBS television, Meadlo said that he had helped to round up about 45 people in the center of the village. "Lieutenant Calley," he recalled, "came over and said, 'You know what to do with them, don't you?' And I said, 'Yes.' So I took it for granted that he just wanted us to watch them. And he left and came back about ten or fifteen minutes later and said, 'How come you ain't killed them yet?' " Whereupon, Meadlo continued, he and Calley shot the civilians with their M-16 rifles. . . . His parents, who joined him on television, were also horrified. "I sent them a good boy," his mother told reporters, "and they made him a murderer."

—"The Killings at Song My," Newsweek, December 8, 1969.

Question: In your opinion, was what happened at My Lai a massacre, an alleged massacre, or what was it, and what do you think can be done to prevent things like this? And if it was a massacre, do you think it was justifiable on military or other grounds?

President Nixon: Well, trying to answer all of those questions . . . I would start first with this statement: What appears was certainly a massacre, and under no circumstances was it justified. One of the goals we are fighting for in Vietnam is to keep the people from South Vietnam from having imposed upon them a Government which has atrocity against civilians as one of its policies, and we cannot ever condone or use atrocities against civilians in order to accomplish that goal. . . .

As far as this kind of activity is concerned, I believe it is an isolated incident. Certainly within this Administration we are doing everything possible to find out whether it was isolated, and so far our investigation indicates that it was. And as far as the future is concerned, I would only add this one point: Looking at the other side of the coin, we have a million, two hundred thousand Americans who have been in Vietnam. Forty thousand of them have given their lives. Virtually all of them have helped the people of Vietnam in one way or another. They built roads and schools, they built churches and pagodas. The Marines alone this year have built over 50,000 churches, pagodas and temples for the people of Vietnam. And our soldiers in Vietnam and sailors and airmen this year alone contributed three-quarters of a million dollars to help the people of South Vietnam.

Now this record of generosity, of decency, must not be allowed to be smeared and slurred because of this kind of an incident. That's why I'm going to do everything I possibly can to see that all the facts in this incident are brought to light, and that those who are charged, if they are found guilty, are punished because if it is isolated it is against our policy and we shall see to it that what these men did—if they did it—does not smear the decent men that have gone to Vietnam in a very, in my opinion, important cause.

—*President Richard Nixon press conference, December 9, 1969.*

DECEMBER 31, 1969:

U.S. Troop Level in South Vietnam—475,200
Total U.S. Killed in Vietnam War—47,765

WASHINGTON, Jan. 22—The prospects for peace in Vietnam were described today by President Nixon as far greater than they were a year ago. He foresaw a good prospect of "a generation of uninterrupted peace" for America.

Mr. Nixon, in his State of the Union Message, drew applause from the joint session of Congress when he said:

"The major immediate goal of our foreign policy is to bring an end to the war in Vietnam in a way that our generation will be remembered not so much as the generation that suffered in the war but more for the fact that we had the courage and character to win the kind of a just peace that the next generation was able to keep."

—*Tad Szulc, "President Terms Prospect for Peace Much Improved,"*
New York Times, *January 23, 1970.*

... **December 15, 1969.** President Nixon announces plans for withdrawal of 50,000 more Americans from South Vietnam by mid-April 1970. . . **January 30, 1970.** President Nixon declares that the "Vietnamization" of the war will continue, regardless of progress at Paris Peace Talks. . . **February 19, 1970.** Chicago 7 defendants are convicted for conspiracy to incite rioting in August 1968 . . . .

SAIGON, South Vietnam, March 14—Many South Vietnamese who live adjacent to areas that are being defoliated by spray from United States planes are convinced that any ailments or misfortunes that they suffer are related to the sprayings.

There is no proof that they are right about the effect of the chemical sprays on the human body, but neither is there any assurance that they are wrong.

Although the defoliation program, organized and run by the United States, has been in operation for nearly nine years, the full effect of the chemicals on animal and human life remains largely undetermined. . . .

A high Agriculture Ministry official said: "I don't think the Americans would use the chemicals if they were harmful."

He conceded that his ministry had made no tests and asserted that his experts had been unable to get any information about the defoliants from the Defense Ministry, which considers such data secret. . . .

Mrs. Tran Thi Tien of Tanhipe, who says she has four normal children, is convinced that the malfunction of her son, who still looks like a newborn at 14 months of age, "must be due to the chemicals I breathed."

Her neighbors, Mrs. Nguyen Thi Hai and Mrs. Tong Thi An, blame the spraying for the fact that their children, one year and 20 months old respectively, still crawl instead of walk.

Nguyen Van Nhap, a farmer, complains of suffering bouts of fever, sneezing and weakness.

"I was working in the field when the spray came down,"

Mrs. Tien said through an interpreter. "I felt dizzy, like vomiting and had to stay in bed three or four days." . . .

Against the psychological drawbacks of the program, United States officials have maintained that the tactical benefits—saving allied lives by denying cover and food to enemy guerrillas—outweighed the liabilities.

> —*Ralph Blumenthal, "U.S. Shows Signs of Concern Over Effect of 9-Year Defoliation Program in Vietnam," New York Times, March 15, 1970.*

Alone among the nations of Indochina, Cambodia had escaped engulfment by war, surviving from one crisis to the next in a precarious state of neutrality nursed along by the nimble diplomacy of a royal ruler. "I'll keep maneuvering as long as I have cards in my hand," Prince Norodom Sihanouk once said. "First a little to the left, then a little to the right. And when I have no more cards to play, I'll stop." Last week, Sihanouk's cards were called by his own hand-picked Parliament, which unanimously ousted the Prince from his job as Cambodia's Chief of State. And, in the wake of this stunning development, diplomats were wondering whether a new game might not be shaping up for Cambodia's warring neighbors as well. . . . Sihanouk charged that his ouster had been engineered by the C.I.A. and hinted that he might try to stage a counter-coup. But whether the Communists would like to see Sihanouk back in power was open to question. For with the Prince out, the way might now be open for the North Vietnamese Army to impose its will on Cambodia.

> —*"From Vietnam to Indochina," Newsweek, March 30, 1970.*

. . . **March 18, 1970.** General Lon Nol overthrows Prince Norodom Sihanouk in Cambodia.

Good evening, my fellow Americans. Ten days ago, in my report to the Nation on Viet-Nam, I announced a decision to withdraw an additional 150,000 Americans from Viet-Nam over the next year. I said then that I was making that decision despite our concern over increased enemy activity in Laos, in Cambodia, and in South Viet-Nam.

At that time, I warned that if I concluded that increased enemy activity in any of these areas endangered the lives of Americans remaining in Viet-Nam I would not hesitate to take strong and effective measures to deal with that situation.

Despite that warning, North Viet-Nam has increased its military aggression in all these areas, and particularly in Cambodia.

After full consultation with the National Security Council, Ambassador Bunker, General Abrams, and my other advisers, I have concluded that the actions of the enemy in the last 10 days clearly endanger the lives of Americans who are in Viet-Nam now and would constitute an unacceptable risk to those who will be there after withdrawal of another 150,000.

To protect our men who are in Viet-Nam and to guarantee the continued success of our withdrawal and the Vietnamization programs, I have concluded that the time has come for action. . . .

In cooperation with the armed forces of South Viet-Nam, attacks are being launched this week to clean out major enemy sanctuaries on the Cambodia–Viet-Nam border. . . . Tonight American and South Vietnamese units will attack the headquarters for the entire Communist military operation in South

. . . **April 1, 1970.** Communists launch new wave of attacks across South Vietnam. . . **April 20, 1970.** President Nixon announces plans to withdraw up to 150,000 Americans from South Vietnam over the next year. . . **April 30, 1970.** President Nixon announces U.S. "incursion" in Cambodia to destroy Communist sanctuaries, sparking nationwide student antiwar strike . . . .

Viet-Nam. This key control center has been occupied by the North Vietnamese and Viet Cong for 5 years in blatant violation of Cambodia's neutrality . . .

If, when the chips are down, the world's most powerful nation, the United States of America, acts like a pitiful, helpless giant, the forces of totalitarianism and anarchy will threaten free nations and free institutions throughout the world . . .

—From President Richard Nixon's televised address to the nation, April 30, 1970.

You know, you see these bums, you know, blowin' up the campuses. Listen, the boys that are on the college campuses today are the luckiest people in the world, going to the greatest universities, and here they are, burnin' up the books, I mean, stormin' around about this issue, I mean, you name it—get rid of the war, there'll be another one.

—President Nixon commenting on antiwar protests, May 1, 1970.

The upheaval in Kent seemed at its outset to be merely another of the scores of student demonstrations that have rocked U.S. campuses. But before it ended, in senseless and brutal murder at point-blank range, Kent State had become a symbol of the fearful hazards latent in dissent, and in the policies that cause it. On cue in the by now familiar scenario, Ohio's Governor James Rhodes ordered the National Guard onto the campus after some 3,000 of Kent State's 20,000 students had rampaged through

. . . **May 4, 1970.** Four students are killed by Ohio National Guardsmen at Kent State University. . . **May 9, 1970.** 100,000 antiwar protesters march in Washington, D.C. . . . . . .

town for two nights smashing windows and setting the ROTC headquarters afire. Then, on a bright Monday noon, students and troops formed skirmish lines, the students fluttering back and forth across the sloping campus in response to the bayoneted thrusts of the soldiers like leaves before the capricious spring winds. Unaware that Ohio, like a few other states, permits its Guardsmen to load live ammunition, the students did not stop pelting the troops with stones, sticks and abuse even when the soldiers lowered and aimed their weapons. One fusillade of high-velocity .30.06 slugs and a clipful of .45s, all steel-jacketed in accord with the articles of war, left four students dead and 11 wounded. The leader of the Guardsmen said his men fired in self-defense, fearing for their lives.

—"*Kent State: Four Deaths at Noon*," Life Magazine, *May 15, 1970.*

Six Guardsmen, including two sergeants and a captain of Troop G, stated pointedly that the lives of the members of the Guard were not in danger and that it was not a shooting situation . . .

We have some reason to believe the claim by the National Guard that their lives were endangered by the students was fabricated subsequent to the event. . . .

Sergeant Robert James of Company A assumed he'd been given an order to fire, so he fired once in the air. As soon as he saw that some of the men of the 107th (Troop G) were firing into the crowd, he ejected his remaining seven shells so he would not fire any more.

Sergeant Richard Love of Company C fired once in the air, then saw others firing into the crowd; he asserted he "could not believe" that the others were shooting into the crowd, so he lowered his weapon.

—*Department of Justice Summary of the FBI Investigation, 1970.*

It is too bad that a small minority of students feel that these damnable demonstrations must take place. If the slouchily dressed female students and the freakishly dressed, long-haired male students would properly dress and otherwise properly demean themselves as not to make show-offs of themselves, such trouble could be and would be avoided. It is difficult to understand why female students must get out and make such fools of themselves as they do, but it is understandable that male students do so largely to get their screwball mugs on television and in the press.

If the troublemaking students have no better sense than to conduct themselves as they do on our university and college campuses, such as throwing missiles, bottles and bullets at legally constituted police authority and the National Guard, they justly deserve the consequences they bring upon themselves, even if this does unfortunately result in death.

—Letter to the editor, The Gazette and Daily, *York, Pennsylvania, May 1970.*

"Bring Us Together"—that was to be the theme of his Administration, Richard Nixon announced the day after he was elected President, and he set about the task with a new-found zest for political conciliation. He courted the South and comforted Middle America until he thought he had conjured up something resembling national unity. Then last week, in one of the most agonizing convulsions the nation has lately endured, Mr. Nixon's short reign of togetherness finally burst apart.

At the sight of a new border crossed in a war they had been told was shrinking, at the sound of a deadly rifle volley loosed by jumpy Ohio National Guardsmen into a crowd of unruly students, a mass of Americans rose up against the President.

Rarely had the nation's citizens seemed so divided, their confidence in its leaders so shaken, their temper so rankled, their young people so driven to desperation and despair. Mr. Nixon had plunged American troops into Cambodia in hopes of shocking the Communist enemy and stabilizing a turbulent world. Instead, he had shocked his fellow countrymen and brought on the most serious domestic crisis of his career.

—"Mr. Nixon's Home Front," Newsweek, May 18, 1970.

By the middle of this week, the last several thousand U.S. troops in Cambodia are scheduled to cross back over the invisible line that divides Cambodia and South Viet Nam, thus bringing the war's most controversial military action to an official end. The national debate that President Nixon's Cambodian decision touched off is certain to continue, however— in the press, in Congress and in the history books. Nixon rendered his own verdict three weeks ago, calling the Cambodia operation the "most successful" military action of the war, a judgment likely to be echoed in his written report to the nation this week. Others, perhaps just as hastily, have compared America's "success" in Cambodia to the results of the *Tet* offensive of 1968, which Lyndon Johnson considered an American victory. *Tet* was, but it also was the decisive point of disenchantment with the war for a substantial number of Americans. . . .

. . . **June 3, 1970.** President Nixon declares that Cambodian invasion was "most successful" military operation of the war, and announces stepped-up U.S. troop withdrawals from South Vietnam. . . **June 24, 1970.** U.S. Senate votes to repeal the Gulf of Tonkin resolution . . . **June 30, 1970.** Last U.S. ground forces withdrawn from Cambodia; bombing continues.

As so often earlier in the long war, the Cambodian decision has set in motion a secondary chain reaction in the U.S. For Richard Nixon, that reaction must seem a negative and not fully foreseen outcome. It has cost him credibility with the people, aroused and angered the Congress and surely limited his future choices in Indochina. Still, by demonstrating to the President the fragility of American public opinion about the war and the deep weariness of the U.S. with any course that does not lead the troops home, the invasion of Cambodia may well, by limiting Nixon's options, ultimately shorten the war. That, of course, was the President's aim in deciding to go into Cambodia in the first place. It is just that it may be working out in ways that he did not expect and would not have chosen.

— *"The Cambodian Venture: An Assessment,"* Time *magazine, July 6, 1970.*

WASHINGTON, Nov. 23—Secretary of Defense Melvin R. Laird disclosed today that a small task force of Army and Air Force men landed about 23 miles west of Hanoi over the weekend in an unsuccessful attempt to free American prisoners thought to be held at a camp there.

The raid, Secretary Laird said at a news conference, was started about 2 A.M. Saturday, Hanoi time. . . .

Secretary Laird said the commando-type raid, which was the first directed at a prisoner-of-war camp in North Vietnam, had

. . . **August 27, 1970.** On visit to Saigon, Vice President Spiro Agnew reaffirms U.S. support for South Vietnam. . . **September 1, 1970.** U.S. Senate rejects McGovern-Hatfield amendment, which would have required withdrawal of all U.S. troops from South Vietnam by the end of 1971. . . **November 21, 1970.** U.S. raid on Son Tay prison camp in North Vietnam fails to find any prisoners to rescue . . . .

been approved by President Nixon after he was told this month that some prisoners were dying.

The raiding party, which landed in helicopters at the prisoner compound at Sontay, discovered that the prisoners had been moved away. . . .

The Government believes that there are 378 American military men held prisoner in North Vietnam. Altogether 780 men are listed as missing in Vietnam, and 1,500 in all of Southeast Asia, some of whom are presumed to be prisoners as well.

> —William Beecher, "U.S. Rescue Force Landed Within 23 Miles of Hanoi, But It Found P.O.W.'s Gone," New York Times, November 24, 1970.

Jimmy Plowman, 3, was born five months after his father was shot down. Plowman is still listed as missing, but a 1967 picture of him in North Vietnam was identified by his parents. His wife is less certain. "It looks so much like Jim," Kathy says, "but the face is swollen. I'm afraid to be too sure of myself." Now the North Vietnamese say Plowman was never captured. Married just two weeks before he went to Vietnam, Kathy recently moved from her parents' home. "Jimmy knows I'm his mother," she explains, "but he was calling my mother mommy and my father daddy. I knew that the older he got, the more difficult it would be."

> —"Memories of Divided Families," Life magazine, December 4, 1970.

. . . **December 10, 1970.** President Nixon warns that he will resume bombing North Vietnam if Communists step up level of attacks in South Vietnam. . . **December 24, 1970.** "Friendly fire" from U.S. artillery kills nine soldiers of the 101st Airborne Division . . . .

DECEMBER 31, 1970:

U.S. Troop Level in South Vietnam—334,600
Total U.S. Killed in Vietnam War—53,849

KHESANH, South Vietnam, Tuesday, Feb. 9—South Vietnamese troops moved into some areas of the enemy's supply-
route network in southern Laos yesterday, hours after having
swept across the border in armored columns and American-
piloted helicopters.

One regiment of the South Vietnamese First Infantry Division, numbering 3,000 soldiers, landed amid a trail complex 20
miles south of the key enemy supply center of Tchepone,
according to Lieut. Col. Thuat Xang, a battalion commander
interviewed here. . . .

Initial enemy resistance in Laos was termed light as South
Vietnamese ground troops advanced across the border from
this northwestern corner of South Vietnam.

> —*Craig R. Whitney, "South Vietnamese Reach Foe's Supply Line in Laos;*
> *2 U.S. Copters Shot Down,"* New York Times, *February 9, 1971.*

For days, the biggest force assembled in South Viet Nam since
Richard Nixon fell heir to the war was poised on the rugged
Laotian frontier. When the signal came from Washington early
last week, hundreds of American helicopters lifted into the

. . . **February 8, 1971.** ARVN troops cross into Laos, in an attack on the Ho Chi Minh Trail,
ending in a debacle for ARVN in late March; some U.S. Marine units participate in attack,
despite Congressional ban on use of U.S. ground combat forces in Laos . . . .

dust-choked sky at Khe Sanh, then darted off to landing zones, where South Vietnamese troops awaited them. At the same time, South Vietnamese tanks and armored personnel carriers rumbled westward on Route 9 and thrust across the border into the jungles of Laos. A new and possibly perilous phase was beginning in the long struggle for Indochina . . .

It was clear that ARVN was finding the going tough. Newsmen saw enough truckloads of ARVN corpses returning from Laos for them to discount official totals of 31 killed and 113 wounded in the first six days. One American Cobra gunship pilot at Khe Sanh said flatly of the South Vietnamese: "They're getting their asses kicked!" That also seemed to apply to South Vietnamese and American flyers, who were encountering some of the most savage anti-aircraft fire of the war.

Reporters also saw some American bodies being brought back from Laos. Was somebody fudging on the congressional curbs on the use of ground troops outside South Viet Nam? White House Press Secretary Ron Ziegler insisted that the reports probably involved Special Forces intelligence teams that have operated in Laos for years. Still, the impression remained that some American advisers had crossed the border.

—"Indochina: The Soft-Sell Invasion," Time magazine, February 22, 1971.

FORT BENNING, Ga., March 30—Gasping for breath, First Lieut. William L. Calley Jr. made a final plea for understanding today as he faced the military jury that convicted him yesterday of the premeditated murder of at least 22 South Vietnamese civilians at Mylai.

. . . **March 29, 1971.** Lt. William Calley convicted of murder for role in My Lai Massacre.

The 5-foot-3-inch platoon leader, who has described himself in an interview as "just a finger, a fragment of a Frankenstein monster," said he never "wantonly" killed anyone. Shaken with sobs, he said the Army never told him that his enemies were human.

The enemy was never described to him as anything but "Communism," he said.

"They [the Army] didn't give it a race, they didn't give it a sex, they didn't give it an age," said Lieutenant Calley, who had been accused by the Government prosecutor of slaying old men, women, children and babies.

> —Homer Bigart, "Calley Pleads for Understanding," New York Times, March 31, 1971.

WASHINGTON, April 7—President Nixon scheduled tonight a withdrawal of 100,000 more American soldiers from South Vietnam by Dec. 1.

The seven-month goal will leave 184,000 American troops in the war zone 11 months before the 1972 Presidential election. Mr. Nixon asked to be held accountable in that election if he failed in his further goal of ending the American involvement in the war.

Addressing the nation on television and radio at a time of widespread restlessness about his war policy, the President said that the invasion of Laos had proved even more damaging to North Vietnam's offensive capacities than the move into Cambodia a year ago.

"Consequently, tonight I can report that Vietnamization has succeeded," Mr. Nixon said.

> —Max Frankel, "Nixon Promises Vietnam Pullout of 100,000 More G.I.'s by December; Pledges to End U.S. Role in War," New York Times, April 8, 1971.

WASHINGTON, APRIL 18—The first contingent of an expected total of 1,500 Vietnam war veterans began arriving here this afternoon in preparation for a week-long series of antiwar protests . . .

The veterans' operation, described as "a limited incursion into the District of Columbia," will begin tomorrow morning with a march from a park near the Jefferson Memorial, where the veterans were spending the night, to the gates of the Arlington National Cemetery across the Potomac River.

The veterans' group had planned a memorial service honoring American and Indochinese war dead at the Tomb of the Unknown Soldier inside the cemetery, but it was refused permission . . .

While in the capital, the group, called the Vietnam Veterans Against the War, will conduct demonstrations at Government agencies, including a "war crimes hearing" at the Capitol.

One organizer said the demonstrations were "the only way left to us to adequately bring home to this country the true story of what has happened in Vietnam."

The plans have run into a number of obstacles from the Nixon Administration. Although the Interior Department gave the group the use of West Potomac Park as an assembly point, it obtained a Federal injunction on Friday to prevent the veterans from using the Federal grounds around the Washington Monument as a sleeping area.

John F. Kerry, a 27-year-old former Navy lieutenant, who is an organizer of the group, said the injunction meant that most of the members, many of whom are unemployed, would have

. . . **April 19–23, 1971.** Vietnam Veterans Against the War (VVAW) stages protests in Washington, D.C.. . . **April 24, 1971.** 500,000 antiwar protesters march in Washington, D.C.

nowhere to sleep during the week because they were unable to afford hotel rooms. . . .

— *"Week of Protests of War to Start,"* New York Times, *April 19, 1971.*

I would like to say for the record, and for the men behind me who are also wearing the uniform and their medals, that my being here is really symbolic. I am not here as John Kerry, but as one member of a group of one thousand, which in turn is a small representation of a very much larger group of veterans in this country . . . I would like to talk about the feelings these men carry with them after coming back from Vietnam . . . In 1970 at West Point Vice President Agnew said, "Some glamorize the criminal misfits of our society while our best men die in Asian rice paddies to preserve the freedom which most of those misfits abuse," and this was used as a rallying point for our effort in Vietnam. But for us, as boys in Asia whom the country was supposed to support, his statement is a terrible distortion from which we can only draw a very deep sense of revulsion, and hence the anger of some of the men who are here in Washington today . . . In our opinion, and from our experience, there is nothing in South Vietnam which could happen that realistically threatens the United States of America. And to attempt to justify the loss of one American life in Vietnam, Cambodia, or Laos by linking such loss to the preservation of freedom . . . is to us the height of criminal hypocrisy . . . Each day to facilitate the process by which the United States washes her hands of Vietnam someone has to give up his life so that the United States doesn't have to admit something that the entire world already knows, so that we can't say that we have made a mistake. Someone has to die so that President Nixon won't be, and these are his words, "the first President to lose a war."

We are asking Americans to think about that because how do you ask a man to be the last man to die in Vietnam? How do you ask a man to be the last man to die for a mistake?

—*John Kerry, former lieutenant (j.g.) U.S. Navy, testimony before the Senate Foreign Relations Committee, April 22, 1971.*

The morale, discipline and battleworthiness of the U.S. Armed Forces are . . . lower and worse than at any time in this century and possibly in the history of the United States.

By every conceivable indicator our army that now remains in Vietnam is in a state approaching collapse—with individual units avoiding or having refused combat, murdering their officers and noncommissioned officers, drug-ridden, and dispirited where not near-mutinous . . .

To understand the military consequences of what is happening to the U.S. Armed Forces, Vietnam is a good place to start. It is in Vietnam that the rearguard of a 500,000-man army, in its day (and in the observation of the writer) the best army the United States ever put into the field, is numbly extricating itself from a nightmare war the Armed Forces feel they had foisted on them by bright civilians who are now back on campus writing books about the folly of it all. . . . "Frag incident" or just "fragging" is current soldier slang in Vietnam for the murder or attempted murder of strict, unpopular or just aggressive officers and NCOs. With extreme reluctance . . . the Pentagon has now disclosed that fraggings in 1970 (209) have more than doubled those of the previous year (96).

. . . **May 3–5, 1971.** Over 12,000 antiwar demonstrators are arrested in "Mayday" demonstrations in Washington, D.C. . . . .

Word of the deaths of officers will bring cheers at troop movies or in bivouacs of certain units.

In one such division—the morale-plagued Americal—fraggings during 1971 have been authoritatively estimated to be running about one a week . . .

Symbolic anti-war fasts (such as the one at Pleiku where an entire medical unit, led by its officers, refused Thanksgiving turkey), peace symbols, "V"-signs not for victory but for peace, booing and cursing of officers and even of hapless entertainers such as Bob Hope, are unhappily common-place. . . .

—*Col. Robert D. Heinl, Jr., USMC, Armed Forces Journal, June 7, 1971.*

WASHINGTON, June 14—Attorney General John N. Mitchell asked *The New York Times* this evening to refrain from further publication of documents drawn from a Pentagon study of the Vietnam war on the ground that such disclosures would cause "irreparable injury to the defense interests of the United States."

If the paper refused, another Justice Department official said, the Government would try to forbid further publication by court action tomorrow.

The *Times* refused to halt publication voluntarily. . . .

In Congress, there were only a few other comments on the matter and no indication that disclosure of the Vietnam materials would significantly influence the Senate vote Wednesday on legislation that would require withdrawal of American forces from the war zone by the end of this year.

Senator George S. McGovern of South Dakota, a cosponsor

. . . **June 13, 1971.** *New York Times* begins publication of "Pentagon Papers" . . . .

of that measure and candidate for the Democratic Presidential nomination, said the documents told a story of "almost incredible deception" of Congress and the American people by the highest officials in Government, including the President.

He said that he did not see how any Senator could ever again believe it was safe to permit the executive branch to make foreign policy alone, and added:

"We would make a serious mistake to assume the kind of deception revealed in these documents began and ended with the Johnson Administration."

> —Max Frankel, "Mitchell Seeks to Halt Series on Vietnam But Times Refuses," New York Times, June 15, 1971.

In recent days, the Federal government has gotten court orders against a number of newspapers to keep them from publishing material from a secret government history of how the U.S. got involved in the war in Vietnam. Do you approve or disapprove of what the government did in this case?

Approve	33%
Disapprove	48%
No opinion	19%

As a general rule, do you think the government tries to keep too much information secret from the public or not?

Yes	56%
No	32%
No opinion	19%

> —Gallup Poll, July 1971.

. . . **June 30, 1971.** U.S. Supreme Court upholds right of *New York Times* and *Washington Post* to publish "Pentagon Papers". . . . .

WASHINGTON, June 30—The Supreme Court freed *The New York Times* and *The Washington Post* today to resume immediate publication of articles based on the secret Pentagon papers on the origins of the Vietnam war.

By a vote of 6 to 3 the Court held that any attempt by the Government to block news articles prior to publication bears "a heavy burden of presumption against its constitutionality."

In a historic test of that principle—the first effort by the Government to enjoin publication on the ground of national security—the Court declared that "the Government has not met that burden."

> —Fred P. Graham, *"Supreme Court, 6–3, Upholds Newspapers on Publication of the Pentagon Report;* Times *Resumes Its Series, Halted 15 Days,"* New York Times, *July 1, 1971.*

Only a free and unrestrained press can effectively expose deception in government. And paramount among the responsibilities of a free press is the duty to prevent any part of the Government from deceiving the people and sending them off to distant lands to die of foreign fevers and foreign shot and shell. In my view, far from deserving condemnation for their courageous reporting, *The New York Times*, *The Washington Post* and other newspapers should be commended for serving the purpose that the Founding Fathers saw so clearly. In revealing the workings of government that led to the Vietnam war, the newspapers nobly did precisely that which the founders hoped and trusted they would do.

> —From Justice Hugo L. Black's concurring opinion in the Supreme Court decision allowing publication of "The Pentagon Papers."

When the *New York Times* and *The Washington Post* resumed publication of the Pentagon papers last week, their substance was no longer electrifying. What passion was left had been expended in the dramatic court battle over publication. Instead, the continued documents now appeared as a sobering elaboration of known or suspected events, the fleshing out of a record increasingly dominated by a single theme.

Time and again, the record portrayed successive U.S. Administrations acting, almost without reassessment, on the conviction that to save South Vietnam from Communism was an overriding national interest. The commitment had arisen first from the intense anti-Communism of the early cold-war years—a time of emerging Communist challenge. Later, roughly at the transition from the Eisenhower to the Kennedy Administrations, it was justified in the conviction that the United States, as the world's greatest power, must never waver in fulfillment of its obligations. The first strategic rationale created the terms of the second. With occasional exceptions, American leaders looked back only to correct the techniques of failure, not to question the established goal. The result was escalation of U.S. involvement, at first slowly, then from 1965 to 1968, at a breakneck pace.

—*"The Secret History of the War (Cont'd),"* Newsweek, July 12, 1971.

Last week, the United States finally admitted what much of the world had known for years: that the Central Intelligence Agency has been supporting a clandestine anti-Communist army in Laos.

A staff report prepared for the Senate Foreign Relations

Committee—and cleared by the CIA, as well as the State and Defense departments—revealed that the U.S. will pay $322 million in the current fiscal year for a 30,000-man irregular army, including Meo tribesmen commanded by Maj. Gen. Vang Pao and 4,000 Thai "volunteers."

—*"Open Secret,"* Newsweek, *August 16, 1971.*

Alongside the broad, American-built expressway between Saigon and Bien Hoa, President Nguyen Van Thieu's eager campaign workers have already hung banners emblazoned with Thieu's "Four Nos" slogan—no neutrality, no coalition government, no concession of any South Vietnamese territory to the Communists, no Communist activity anywhere in South Viet Nam. Thieu might as well have added a Fifth No: no opposition in the presidential campaigns.

With only five weeks remaining until South Viet Nam's October election, there was still no end in sight to the political snafu that has become at once a bitter joke in cynical Saigon and a source of deep embarrassment to Washington. So long as Thieu held the lines of governmental power and could steer the results in his favor, neither retired General Duong Van ("Big") Minh nor South Viet Nam's feisty Vice President Nguyen Cao Ky would consent to run as opposition candidates. That left Thieu the sole contender, knocking the underpinnings from the U.S. contention that it remains in South Viet Nam at the request of a freely and democratically elected government.

—*"South Viet Nam's Fifth No,"* Time *magazine, September 6, 1971.*

Demonstrations, petitions and election are part of the lifeblood of a democracy. And South Vietnam, which masquerades as a democracy, has all three. Two weeks ago, a group of lower-house deputies demonstrated on the steps of Vietnam's National Assembly, but they were tear-gassed by riot police. Last week, the Vietnamese Senate passed a resolution, 28 to 3, but it was ignored. And next week there will be a Presidential election—but it involves only one candidate, President Nguyen Van Thieu.

Once there was a chance that this election could have marked a turning point for this exhausted country, a chance for millions of South Vietnamese to make a real choice about their future at the ballot box. The tear-gassed deputies and the Senate petitioners both wanted the election postponed, to allow another candidate to enter the race. But Thieu refused, and his one-man election adds yet another U.S.-sanctioned scandal to a list that already includes the Tonkin Gulf incident, My Lai and rampant heroin addiction.

—Kevin Buckley, "The Puppet Pulls the Strings," Newsweek, October 4, 1971.

DECEMBER 31, 1971:

U.S. Troop Level in South Vietnam—156,800
Total U.S. Killed in Vietnam War—56,205

At last the three years of secret diplomacy, the seven months of public anticipation, and the frantic final hours of official prepa-

. . . **October 3, 1971.** President Thieu is re-elected in a one-man race for the presidency of South Vietnam. . . **December 26, 1971.** U.S. planes bomb airfields and other installations in North Vietnam in heaviest attacks since suspension of bombing in 1968. . . **January 25, 1972.** President Nixon reveals secret peace negotiations between Henry Kissinger and Le Duc Tho. . . **February 21, 1972.** President Nixon arrives in Peking . . . .

ration were over. The doors had swung open on a new policy of dialogue between China and the U.S., two world powers that had refused to talk to each other for nearly 25 years. Despite the President's repeated comparison of his trip to the *Apollo 11* flight, Peking is too much a part of this world to be the moon, and a presidential jet is far safer and more comfortable than a space capsule. Yet this too was a historic adventure, an uncertain portent for mankind's future . . .

Although Nixon was to set foot in China during a 50-minute rest and refueling stop in Shanghai, where he would pick up a Chinese navigator, interpreter and radio operator for the 710-mile final leg to Peking, the first public ceremony was to be at Peking airport. Conveniently timed for mass TV viewing Sunday night in the U.S.—Monday morning in Peking—this would be the first of the television spectaculars on a mission in which television rated a high priority in the White House planning. Although the White House refused to confirm any details, it was certain that Premier Chou En-lai would meet Nixon at the airport, and the TV screen then would record a strange sight: Nixon, the champion of capitalism, riding with Chou in an official black Hongchi (*Red Flag*) car and entering Tienanmen Square. There they would pass the ancient scarlet walls of China's imperial past and the Gate of Heavenly Peace from which Chairman Mao Tse-tung in 1949 proclaimed the birth of the People's Republic.

> —*"Now, in Living Color from China,"* Time *magazine, February 28, 1972.*

. . . **March 23, 1972.** U.S. suspends Paris Peace Talks. . . **March 30, 1972.** North Vietnamese launch new offensive, the heaviest since 1968. . . **April 6, 1972.** Expanded U.S. air strikes against North Vietnamese troops in South Vietnam launched; mission is codenamed Operation Linebacker . . . .

One of the major lessons of the war in Indochina has been the futility of trying to anticipate Hanoi. Time and again, U.S. strategists have sought to read the mind of the North Vietnamese high command and, more often than not, their predictions have proved wrong. Yet early last week, the crystal-ball gazers were at it again. Their newest theory was that the recent suspension of the Paris peace talks by the U.S. and a series of battlefield victories by the South Vietnamese Army had thrown Hanoi off its stride. But no sooner had this optimistic assessment begun to make the rounds than Hanoi literally shot it full of holes.

In their heaviest attack in more than four years, the Communists last week struck savagely at South Vietnamese bases and villages along the demilitarized zone that separates the two Vietnams. Combining a massive bombardment with ground assaults, the enemy rained some 12,000 rounds of artillery, rocket and mortar shells down upon a chain of South Vietnamese bases that guard the DMZ. It was the biggest Communist assault since the artillery siege of the Khe Sanh Marine base in January 1968, and beneath its fury the defenders gave way. With tanks spearheading their assault, the Communists overran all but one base camp, including Fuller, Holcomb and Charlie 2. And as South Vietnamese troops retreated, the attackers pushed within 5 miles of the provincial capital of Quang Tri. At the same time, the enemy launched attacks against government positions in the central highlands and in Tay Ninh Province northwest of Saigon. Said a U.S. analyst: "Those theoreticians ought to ask the guys at the fire-support bases that got clobbered last week if they think Hanoi is on the defensive."

—*"Hanoi Attacks—and Blasts a Dream,"* Newsweek, April 10, 1972.

HUE, South Vietnam, May 5—The young American helicopter pilot, rescued by another helicopter after having been shot down by North Vietnamese ground fire, was badly cut and bruised and in a state of shock.

"It's a dream. It's a dream," he kept repeating incredulously. "It's not happening to me. It's happening to someone else and he's got inside me."

With his words of stunned disbelief, he could have been talking about what happened on the whole northern front this past week—an entire South Vietnamese division was put to rout, thousands of soldiers deserted and went on drunken looting sprees, and tens of thousands of civilians fled southward to escape the enemy advance, leaving Hue a city of empty streets and nervous soldiers.

> —*Sydney H. Schanberg, "Reporter's Notebook: Victims of Onslaught Living in Fear, Bewilderment and Despair," New York Times, May 8, 1972.*

It is plain then that what appears to be a choice among three courses of action for the United States is really no choice at all. The killing in this tragic war must stop. By simply getting out, we would only worsen the bloodshed. By relying solely on negotiations, we would give an intransigent enemy the time he needs to press his aggression on the battlefield.

There is only one way to stop the killing. That is to keep the

---

... **April 15, 1972.** U.S. renews bombing of Hanoi and Haiphong for the first time since 1968; for the first time B-52s are used to attack targets near the cities. . . **April 17, 1972.** Campus protests spread against the renewed fighting in Vietnam. . . **April 27, 1972.** Paris Peace Talks resume. . . **May 1, 1972.** Quang Tri falls to North Vietnamese. . . **May 8, 1972.** President Nixon announces mining of North Vietnamese ports . . . .

weapons of war out of the hands of the international outlaws of North Vietnam. . . .

I therefore concluded that Hanoi must be denied the weapons and supplies it needs to continue the aggression. In full coordination with the Republic of Vietnam, I have ordered the following measures which are being implemented as I am speaking to you.

All entrances to North Vietnamese ports will be mined to prevent access to these ports and North Vietnamese naval operations from these ports. United States forces have been directed to take appropriate measures within the internal and claimed territorial waters of North Vietnam to interdict the delivery of supplies. Rail and all other communications will be cut off to the maximum extent possible. Air and naval strikes against military targets in North Vietnam will continue. . . .

These actions I have ordered will cease when the following conditions are met:

First, all American prisoners of war must be returned.

Second, there must be an internationally supervised cease-fire throughout Indochina.

Once prisoners of war are released, once the internationally supervised cease-fire has begun, we will stop all acts of force throughout Indochina, and at that time we will proceed with a complete withdrawal of all American forces from Vietnam within 4 months.

Now these terms are generous terms. They are terms which would not require surrender and humiliation on the part of anybody. They would permit the United States to withdraw with honor. They would end the killing. They would bring our POW's home. They would allow negotiations on a political settlement between the Vietnamese themselves. They would permit all the nations which have suffered in this long war—

Cambodia, Laos, North Vietnam, South Vietnam—to turn at last to the urgent works of healing and of peace. They deserve immediate acceptance by North Vietnam.

—*From Richard Nixon's televised address to the nation, May 8, 1972.*

WASHINGTON, May 8—President Nixon's speech tonight appealed to the Soviet Union not to let its support of Hanoi lead it to a confrontation with the United States over his decision to try to cut off supplies to North Vietnam.

In carefully chosen language, Mr. Nixon appeared anxious to avoid turning the Vietnam war into a direct Soviet-American clash.

But some diplomats feel the mining of North Vietnam's ports has raised the possibility of cancellation of Mr. Nixon's scheduled trip to Moscow two weeks from today and even of a military confrontation if Soviet naval forces try to thwart Mr. Nixon's actions.

—*Bernard Gwertzman, "President Urges Soviets To Avoid Confrontation," New York Times, May 9, 1992.*

"I was keyed up and ready for battle as the flight neared Moscow," Richard Nixon wrote of his first trip to the Soviet Union thirteen years ago. And battle he did with Nikita Khrushchev in that famous kitchen debate. But times have changed and so has Richard Nixon. Now that he has reopened the door to China, the old cold warrior sets out this week on the second leg of his peace-seeking odyssey to the Communist camp. And

. . . **May 20, 1972.** President Nixon meets with Soviet leaders in Moscow. . . . .

as if to prove that coexistence has finally come of age, the President and Soviet Communist Party chief Leonid Brezhnev meet at the summit in Moscow while U.S. planes and Soviet tanks are locked in brutal combat 5,000 miles away in Indochina.

—*"Moscow Summit,"* Newsweek, *May 29, 1972.*

Suddenly a roar went up in the convention hall, louder than anything I had ever heard in my life. It started off as a rumble, then gained in intensity until it sounded like a tremendous thunderbolt. "Four more years, four more years," the crowd roared over and over again. The fat woman next to me was jumping up and down and dancing in the aisle. It was the greatest ovation the President of the United States had ever received and he loved it. I held the sides of my wheelchair to keep my hands from shaking. After what seemed forever, the roar finally began to die down.

This was the moment I had come three thousand miles for, this was it, all the pain and the rage, all the trials and the death of the war and what had been done to me and a generation of Americans by all the men who had lied to us and tricked us, by the man who stood up before us in the convention hall that night, while men who had fought for their country were being gassed and beaten in the street outside the hall. I thought of Bobby who sat next to me and the months we had spent in the [VA] hospital in the Bronx. It was all hitting me at once, all those years, all that destruction, all that sorrow.

President Nixon began to speak and all three of us took a deep breath and shouted at the top of our lungs, "Stop the bombing, stop the war, stop the bombing, stop the war," as loud and as hard as we could, looking directly at Nixon. The security agents immediately threw up their arms, trying to hide us from the cameras and the president. "Stop the bombing, stop the bombing," I screamed. For an instant [Walter] Cronkite looked down, then turned his head away. They're not going to show it, I thought. They're going to try and hide us like they did in the hospitals. Hundreds of people around us began to clap and shout, "Four more years," trying to drown out our protest. They all seemed very angry and shouted at us to stop. We continued shouting, interrupting Nixon again and again until Secret Service agents grabbed our chairs from behind and began pulling us backward as fast as they could out of the convention hall . . .

A short guy with a big "Four More Years" button ran up to me and spat in my face. "Traitor!" he screamed, as he was yanked back by police. Pandemonium was breaking out all around us and the Secret Service men kept pulling us out backward.

"I served two tours of duty in Vietnam!" I screamed to one newsman. "I gave three-quarters of my body for America. And what do I get? Spit in the face!" I kept screaming until we hit the side entrance where the agents pushed us outside and shut the doors, locking them with chains and padlocks so reporters wouldn't be able to follow us out for interviews.

All three of us sat holding on to each other shaking. We had done it. It had been the biggest moment of our lives, we had shouted down the President of the United States and disrupted his acceptance speech. What more was there left to do but go home?

I sat in my chair still shaking and began to cry.

—*Sgt. Ron Kovic, USMC,* Born on the Fourth of July *(1976).*

. . . **June 17, 1972.** Five men are arrested breaking into Democratic National Committee headquarters in Washington, D.C., the beginning of the "Watergate scandal" which will destroy Richard Nixon's presidency. . . . .

The Provisional Revolutionary Government of the Republic of South Vietnam solemnly declares as follows:

If a correct solution is to be found to the Vietnam problem, and a lasting peace ensured in Vietnam, the U.S. Government must meet the two following requirements:

1—To respect the Vietnamese people's right to true independence and the South Vietnamese people's right to effective self-determination; stop the U.S. war of aggression in Vietnam, the bombing, mining and blockade of the Democratic Republic of Vietnam; completely cease the "Vietnamization" policy; end all U.S. military activities in South Vietnam; rapidly and completely withdraw all U.S. troops, advisers, military personnel, technical personnel, weapons and war materials and those of the other foreign countries in the U.S. camp from South Vietnam; liquidate the U.S. military bases in South Vietnam; end all U.S. military involvement in Vietnam; and stop supporting the Nguyen Van Thieu stooge administration.

2—A solution to the internal problem of South Vietnam must proceed from the actual situation that exists in South Vietnam: two administrations, two armies, and other political forces. It is necessary to achieve national concord. The sides in South Vietnam must unite on the basis of equality, mutual respect and mutual nonelimination. Democratic freedoms must be guaranteed to the people. To this end, it is necessary to form in South Vietnam a provisional government of national concord with three equal segments to take charge of the affairs in the period of transition and to organize truly free and democratic general elections.

—Statement of the Provisional Revolutionary Government (PRG) of South Vietnam, September 11, 1972.

... **September 15, 1972.** Quang Tri recaptured by South Vietnamese after four-and-a-half-month battle. . . . .

We believe that peace is at hand. We believe that an agreement is within sight.

—*Secretary of State Henry Kissinger, October 26, 1972.*

CHICAGO, Nov. 3—Senator George McGovern charged tonight that President Nixon had only "pretended" to be near a negotiated settlement of the Vietnam war. He said the President's actions were part of a re-election strategy based on "cruel political deception."

The Democratic Presidential nominee, using blunt and at times bitter language, declared in a nationally televised address that Mr. Nixon had "closed the door to peace once again" by refusing to accept without refinement the settlement that his own Administration had negotiated with North Vietnam.

—*James M. Naughton, "McGovern Asserts Nixon Pretended to Be Near Peace," New York Times, November 4, 1972.*

SAN CLEMENTE, Calif. Nov. 6—President Nixon spent the last few moments of his re-election campaign tonight defending himself against Senator George McGovern's charge that he had deceived the American people about the prospects for a settlement in Vietnam.

In a five-minute nationwide television statement, Mr. Nixon said he had achieved a "breakthrough" in the negotiations and

. . . **October 8, 1972.** Intensive top-level negotiations in Paris lead to speculation of imminent peace agreement. . . **October 17, 1972.** Henry Kissinger flies to Saigon for meeting with President Thieu. . . **October 26, 1972.** Kissinger announces that peace agreement "is in sight". . . . .

that both Hanoi and the United States had agreed on a cease-fire, a return of all prisoners of war and a political settlement under which "the people of South Vietnam will determine their own future."

Mr. Nixon said there remained "some details that we are insisting still be worked out" because he wished to be certain "that this will not be a temporary peace but a peace that will last."

But he said he was "completely confident" that he would soon reach an agreement "which will end the war in Vietnam."

—*Robert B. Semple, Jr., "Nation Will Vote Today, Nixon Favored to Defeat M'Govern by Wide Margin, President Rebuts Charge,"* New York Times, *November 7, 1972.*

PRESIDENTIAL ELECTION, 1972:

Candidate	Party	% of Popular Vote
Richard M. Nixon	Republican	60.7
George S. McGovern	Democratic	37.5

Six years have passed since the Vietnam war brought its first death to Massillon [Ohio] . . . In the interim, what seems like a whole generation has grown up, gone to work in the steel mills, bought houses and started families. Many of Massillon's young men have gone into the armed forces, some to Vietnam. But last week hardly anybody—even at the VFW or American Legion—knew for sure how many actually lost their lives there. The figure is 13. And now, the prospect of peace is

. . . **November 7, 1972.** President Nixon defeats George McGovern for presidency. . . . . . .

unmarked by celebration, and the real cost of the war is being forgotten by people absorbed with everyday matters: unemployment, inflation, a new car or the high school football team. The families of those killed or missing or taken prisoner suffer; but in Massillon, as in most of the U.S., they do so silently.

—*"No Bells for Peace,"* Life *magazine, November 10, 1972.*

It was a hazard that even Henry Kissinger may have overlooked. As a result of the long delay in clinching Mr. Nixon's deal with Hanoi, many Americans had a chance to take a careful look at the fine print in the agreement. What they discovered was that although the deal gave the U.S. a discreet fig leaf to cover its withdrawal it was hardly calculated to assure a lasting peace in South Vietnam. Both in military and political terms, the agreement was at once too complex and too vague. Thus, even if Kissinger managed to clarify all the current sticking points with the North Vietnamese, the terms of the accord left many people wondering whether the U.S. had merely set the stage for an inevitable third Indochina war.

—*"A Third Vietnamese War?",* Newsweek, *November 13, 1972.*

I don't want any more of this crap about the fact that we couldn't hit this target or that one. This is your chance to use military power to win this war, and if you don't I'll hold you responsible.

—*President Richard M. Nixon to Admiral Thomas Moorer, Chairman of the Joint Chiefs of Staff, ordering renewed air attacks on Hanoi and Haiphong, December 14, 1972.*

. . . **December 18–29, 1972.** Blaming Hanoi for delay in reaching final peace agreement, President Nixon launches Operation Linebacker II, the "Christmas bombing" of Hanoi and Haiphong . . . .

WASHINGTON, Dec. 18—The Nixon Administration announced a resumption of full-scale bombing and mining of North Vietnam today, and the White House warned that such raids "will continue until such time as a settlement is arrived at."

Administration officials said that President Nixon, in ordering actions against military objectives in the Hanoi and Haiphong areas, had directed the Air Force and Navy to strike targets not bombed before.

United States officials in Saigon said hundreds of planes, including B-52's, resumed attacks above the 20th parallel in North Vietnam, carrying out the heaviest raids of the war in the Hanoi-Haiphong region . . .

—William Beecher, "White House Says Raiding in the North Will Go on Until There is an Accord," New York Times, December 19, 1972.

STOCKHOLM, Dec. 22—Hanoi's largest hospital, one mile west of the city center, was damaged by American planes early today, according to the Swedish foreign ministry.

It said Sweden's charge d'affaires in Hanoi, Eskil Lundberg, had reported by radiophone that the 1,000-bed Bach Mai Hospital had been hit between 4 and 6 A.M. . . . Mr. Lundberg, who spoke with Sweden's Ambassador to North Vietnam, Jean Christophe Oeberg, now in Stockholm for the holiday, reported that a press party had been taken to the scene . . . Mr. Oeberg said Mr. Lundberg had reported that since the beginning of the B-52 raids on North Vietnam on Monday, a third of Hanoi's hospital facilities had been destroyed. In addition, according to Mr. Oeberg, the charge d'affaires had said that American bombs had fallen in densely populated areas, heavily damaging parts of central Hanoi that had not been hit before.

> —*"Largest Hospital in Hanoi Reported Damaged in Raid,"* New York
> Times, *December 23, 1972.*

DECEMBER 31, 1972:

U.S. Troop Level in South Vietnam—24,000
Total U.S. Killed in Vietnam War—56,845

WASHINGTON, Jan. 23—President Nixon said tonight that Henry A. Kissinger and North Vietnam's chief negotiator, Le Duc Tho, had initialed an agreement in Paris today "to end the war and bring peace with honor in Vietnam and Southeast Asia."

In a televised report to the nation, a few hours after Mr. Kissinger returned to Washington, Mr. Nixon said a cease-fire in Vietnam would go into effect on Saturday at 7 P.M., Eastern Standard time. . . .

Mr. Nixon said that under the terms of the accord—which will be formally signed on Saturday—all American prisoners of war would be released and the remaining 23,700-man American force in South Vietnam would be withdrawn within 60 days.

> —*Bernard Gwertzman, "Vietnam Accord is Reached; Cease-Fire Begins
> Saturday; P.O.W.'s to be Free in 60 Days,"* New York Times, *January
> 24, 1973.*

WASHINGTON, Jan. 23—America is moving out of Vietnam after the longest and most divisive conflict since the War Between the States. But Vietnam is not moving out of America, for the impact of the war is likely to influence American life for many years to come. Though it is probably too early to distinguish between the temporary and the enduring consequences, one thing is fairly clear: There has been a sharp decline in respect for authority in the United States as a result of the war—a decline in respect not only for the civil authority of government, but also for the moral authority of the schools, the universities, the press, the church and even the family.

There was no cease-fire on this front.

> —James Reston, "War Leaves Deep Mark on U.S.," New York Times, January 24, 1973.

We have finally achieved peace with honor.

> —President Richard M. Nixon, January 27, 1973.

Pretty soon we begin hearing Hanoi Hannah talk about the Paris Peace Accords, which had been signed on the twenty-seventh of January. A short time after that we get our own personal copy of the protocol pertaining to POWs, wherein it states that no later than the twelfth of February of '73, a minimum of one-fourth of the POWs will be released. While we're waiting, Colonel Risner, who's then the ranking POW in Camp Unity, tells the camp commander how we want the releases to be done: sick and injured first, followed by shoot-down order beginning with Alvarez, from August of '64. I

. . . **January 27, 1973.** Signing of Paris Peace Accords ends direct U.S. military role in South Vietnam conflict . . . .

think from my shootdown date I'll probably be in the first group.

The North Vietnamese start giving us large quantities of food. Fish, rice, bread, sugar, in an obvious attempt to fatten us up. We go along with it. They open up the rooms first thing in the morning, and they're open that way all day. Playing volleyball. Finally, after all these years, the twelfth of February arrives, and I am in the first group. . . .

We lined up in shootdown order. They called out my name. I stepped forward. There was a colonel. I saluted him and said, "Good to be back." He shook my hand and said, "Congratulations, glad to have you back." We stepped another twenty feet and there was another colonel. I saluted him. He turned me over to an air-crew member, who escorted me to the [C-141 transport plane]. He had to hold on very tight to my arm, because I was so emotional. As I began walking to the plane, I had reporters sticking microphones in my face and asking me questions, which I could not answer. I was all choked up, but it was too exciting to cry. As I got closer and closer to that 141, I looked up at the tail and saw a big red cross painted on it. On top of that red cross was a big, beautiful American flag.

> —*Colonel Jerry Driscoll, USAF, quoted in Harry Maurer,* Strange Ground: Americans in Vietnam, 1945–1975, An Oral History *(1989). [Driscoll was shot down over North Vietnam and captured in April 1966.]*

. . . **February 21, 1973.** Peace agreement signed in Laos, ends U.S. bombing. . . **March 29, 1973.** All known U.S. prisoners of war have now been returned. . . **June 24, 1973.** Graham Martin is appointed U.S. Ambassador to South Vietnam. . . **July 1, 1973.** U.S. Congress sets cutoff for U.S. bombing of Cambodia by August 15, 1973 . . . .

SEC. 108. Nothwithstanding any other provision of law, on or after August 15, 1973, no funds herein or heretofore appropriated may be obligated or expended to finance directly or indirectly combat activities by United States military forces in or over or from off the shores of North Vietnam, South Vietnam, Laos or Cambodia.

—*Fulbright-Aiken Amendment, Public Law 93-52, Section 108, July 1, 1973.*

DECEMBER 31, 1973:

U.S. Troop Levels in South Vietnam—50
Total U.S. Killed in Vietnam War—57,011

6

THE PARIS PEACE ACCORDS did not end the fighting in South Vietnam. Both sides were soon back on the offensive. In the spring of 1975 the Communists launched a military attack in the northern provinces and central highlands of South Vietnam, which turned into a rout of South Vietnamese forces. Hue and Da Nang fell to the Communists; by the start of April they controlled more than half the country. Thieu and other South Vietnamese leaders fled for safety to the United States. On April 29th–30th helicopters carried the last remaining American personnel out of Saigon. Two American marines died during the operation, the last U.S. casualties of the war. As Communist tanks and troops entered Saigon, the war came to an end.

In the years that followed, Americans tried to come to grips with the Vietnam experience. Some, like former President Richard Nixon, argued that if Americans had shown more willpower and unity at home, the U.S. military would eventually have prevailed in Vietnam. Others argued that Vietnam proved the folly of the U.S. attempting to act as the world's policeman. The dedication of the Vietnam War Memorial in Washington, D.C., in 1982 was taken by many as a symbol of national reconciliation, as well as a long overdue tribute to the more than 58,000 Americans whose names are inscribed on the black marble walls of the monument.

AFTERMATH

We won the war but we lost the peace. All that we had achieved in twelve years of fighting was thrown away in a spasm of congressional irresponsibility.

—*Richard M. Nixon,* No More Vietnams *(1985).*

Kissinger and others have suggested that Watergate, by turning Congress against Nixon, spelled the end for Indochina. But the argument is simplistic. The Watergate scandal did indeed ruin Nixon, thereby propelling Congress into asserting its prerogatives in foreign policy, as frequently occurs when the executive branch is weakened. But given the public's antipathy towards Vietnam at the time, it is doubtful that the United States could have regenerated a commitment to rescue Thieu's government.

—*Stanley Karnow,* Vietnam: A History *(1983).*

August 9, 1974. President Richard Nixon resigns. . . **August 20, 1974.** U.S. Congress cuts level of aid to South Vietnam. . . **March 10, 1975.** Ban Me Thuot falls to North Vietnamese . . . **March 14, 1975.** South Vietnamese President Nguyen Van Thieu orders withdrawal of South Vietnamese military forces from northern provinces. . . **March 26, 1975.** Hue falls to North Vietnamese. . . **March 30, 1975.** Da Nang falls to North Vietnamese. . . **April 12, 1975.** President Thieu resigns . . . .

April 30 [1975]:

Day came suddenly, but the terrors of the night did not vanish.

In the livid light of dawn Saigon was a ghost city. Huge gray clouds rolled slowly over the silent extension of houses, buildings, monuments, and hovels, and were lost in the limpid remoteness of the sea that no one could reach any longer.

It was as though an unforeseen pestilence had swept away three million inhabitants. Large rats scoured through piles of sweetish, putrid garbage on the sidewalks. Every so often a jeep full of soldiers crept along the wet pavement of the broad avenues, their rifles leveled at the shuttered stores, the bolted doors and windows. Gusts of wind raised eddies of waste paper and scattered packets of documents, newspapers, and letters left on the streets by the looters.

Only around the American embassy was there still turmoil. At 7:30 the Marines standing guard at the outside wall retired, in battle formation, their bayonets pointed at a desperate crowd of Vietnamese who were now climbing over the gate, invading the lawn, and bursting with shouts into the building to rob and destroy. The retreating Marines ran along the roof, firing tear gas into the stairwells. Other Marines went to the safe, sprinkled a can of gasoline on the piles of hundred-dollar bills constituting the funds of the embassy, and set them on fire. . . .

On the floor of the lobby, near the plaque commemorating the Marines who had died defending the embassy during the Tet offensive, lay a sentence from Lawrence of Arabia that

---

... **April 17, 1975.** Cambodian Communist Khmer Rouge forces capture Phnompenh
... **April 29, 1975.** Two U.S. servicemen are killed by North Vietnamese rocket in Saigon, the last of 47,244 Americans killed in action in the Vietnam War... **April 30, 1975.** Communist forces capture Saigon, ending the Vietnam War. . . . .

American military advisers loved to recite and which someone in the embassy had had framed:

"It is better that they do it imperfectly than that you do it perfectly. For it is their war and their country and your time here is limited."

At 7:45 a green helicopter alighted on the roof. The last eleven Marines flung themselves through the open doors and the helicopter lifted off. . . .

From a nearby house at the lower end of Thong Nhat Avenue, ARVN soldiers discharged their rage and their machine guns at the iron belly hovering in the gray sky. The helicopter swerved abruptly and they missed it. The sound of the churning blades dissolved in the damp sultry morning air, and a moment later the helicopter was a diminishing speck on the horizon. It was the last. The last.

—*Tiziano Terzani,* Giai Phong! The Fall and Liberation of Saigon *(1976).*

When the North Vietnamese struck, in March of 1975, a sort of shudder ran through South Vietnamese society from top to bottom. Like a building that hangs suspended in midair for a split second after its foundations have been dynamited, the government of South Vietnam remained standing briefly, and began to go through motions of responding; then it flew to pieces. . . . Within a few days of the attack, President Thieu made a ruinous decision to in effect abandon large portions of the northern section of South Vietnam by withdrawing the troops there farther south. These troops, judged unable to defend their territory by their commander, soon proved incapable even of retreating. Instead they disintegrated as a fighting force . . . Soon the pandemonium of the retreat spread to the society at large. . . . South Vietnamese soldiers, far from fighting the enemy, began to battle one another and shoot civilians . . . As for fighting between the opposing armies, it was rare. In the words of one American official on the scene, there was "no war." . . . With the exception of a few engagements in which units of the South Vietnamese Army stood and fought, the same pattern repeated itself throughout the country . . .

The collapse of South Vietnam revealed its true nature, and with it, the true nature of the war. It was a society entirely without inner cohesion, held together only by foreign arms, foreign money, foreign political will.

—*Jonathan Schell,* The Real War *(1988).*

Today, America can regain the sense of pride that existed before Vietnam. But it cannot be achieved by refighting a war that is finished . . . These events, tragic as they are, portend neither the end of the world nor of America's leadership in the world.

—*President Gerald R. Ford, May 7, 1975.*

What we need now in this country, for some weeks at least, and hopefully for some months, is to . . . put Vietnam behind us and to concentrate on problems of the future.

—*Secretary of State Henry Kissinger, April 29, 1975.*

Today it is almost as though the war had never happened. Americans have somehow blocked it out of their conscious-

ness. They don't talk about it. They don't talk about the consequences.

—*Joseph C. Harsch, "Do You Recall Vietnam—And What About the
Dominoes?" Louisville Courier-Journal, October 2, 1975.*

San Francisco airport—
no more corpsmen stuffing ruptured chests
with cotton balls and not enough heat tabs
to eat a decent meal.

I asked some girl to sit
and have a Coke with me.
She thought I was crazy;
I thought she was going to call a cop.

I bought a ticket for Philadelphia.
At the loading gate, they told me:
"Thank you for flying TWA;
We hope you will enjoy your flight."

No brass bands;
no flags,
no girls,
no cameramen.

Only a small boy who asked me
what the ribbons on my jacket meant.

—*Sgt. William Ehrhart, USMC, The Awkward Silence [1980].*

I was never spit on. I was never spat at. I never have talked to
any other vet who was. Someone always claims to know someone else who was—and always at the airport. Like most other
things concerning Vietnam, I think it was probably blown out of

proportion. Most people really just didn't give a damn whether you were there or not, and I think most people still don't.

—*Steven Gist [who served with the Marines in Vietnam in 1967], quoted in Bob Greene,* Homecoming: When The Soldiers Returned From Vietnam *(1989).*

The era of self-doubt is over.

—*President Ronald Reagan speech to West Point cadets, May 27, 1981.*

If I recall correctly, when France gave up Indochina as a colony, the leading nations of the world met in Geneva in regard to helping those colonies become independent nations. And since North and South Vietnam had been previous to colonization two separate countries, provisions were made that these two countries could by a vote of all their people together decide whether they wanted to be one country or not . . .

And there wasn't anything surreptitious about it, but when Ho Chi Minh refused to participate in such an election and there was provision that the peoples of both countries could cross the border and live in the other country if they wanted to, and when they began leaving by the thousands and thousands from North Vietnam to live in South Vietnam, Ho Chi Minh closed the border and again violated that part of the agreement . . .

—*President Ronald Reagan, press conference, April 1982.*

The Vietnam War was a limited war, with limited objectives, prosecuted by limited means, with limited public support. Therefore, it was destined to be (and was) a long war, a war so long that public support waned and political decisions by Congress terminated our involvement, resulting in a victory by the North Vietnamese Communists.

The military did not lose a battle of consequence and did not lose the war. The war was lost by congressional actions withdrawing support to the South Vietnamese government despite commitments by President Nixon.

—General William C. Westmoreland, quoted in "What Shall We Tell Our Children About Vietnam?", American Heritage, May/June 1988.

Following the war, still perplexed by his failure, Westmoreland said, "Any American commander who took the same vast losses as [North Vietnamese military commander General Vo Nguyen] Giap would have been sacked overnight."

But Giap was not an American among strange people in a faraway land. His troops and their civilian supporters were fighting on their own soil, convinced that their sacrifices would erode the patience of their foes and, over time, bring Vietnam under Communist control. He had used this strategy against France, and he was confident that it would work against the United States.

"We were not strong enough to drive out a half-million American troops, but that wasn't our aim," he told me. "Our intention was to break the will of the American Government to continue the war. Westmoreland was wrong to expect that his superior firepower would grind us down. If we had focused on the balance of forces, we would have been defeated in two hours. We were waging a people's war—à la manière vietnamiene. America's sophisticated arms, electronic devices and all the rest were to no avail in the end. In war there are the two factors—human beings and weapons. Ultimately, though, human beings are the decisive factor. Human beings! Human beings!"

—*Stanley Karnow, "Giap Remembers," New York Times Magazine, June 24, 1990.*

The United States must be careful not to interpret events occurring in a different land in terms of its own history, politics, culture, and morals.

—*Robert S. McNamara [Secretary of Defense 1961–67], quoted in "What Should We Tell Our Children About Vietnam?", American Heritage, May/June 1988.*

1990 Gallup Poll results:

Looking back, do you think the United States made a mistake sending troops to fight in Vietnam?

Yes 74%

Some people say that the United States should have cut its losses by accepting a negotiated withdrawal from Vietnam much earlier than it did. Others say the United States should have made an even greater military effort to try to win a victory there. Which comes closer to your view?

Withdrawn earlier 56%
Made greater military effort 38%
No opinion 6%

The spectre of Vietnam has been buried forever in the desert sands of the Arabian peninsula.

—*President George Bush, radio address in the aftermath of the Persian Gulf War victory, March 1991.*

There was such a dense concentration of American energy there, American and essentially adolescent, if that energy could have been channeled into anything more than noise, waste and pain it would have lighted up Indochina for a thousand years.

—*Michael Herr,* Dispatches *(1978).*

Total U.S. Killed in Vietnam War 1959–1975—58,169